AVIATION POCKET GUIDE 6

AIR

The Ai

of t

G000123304

Graeme and Brian Pickering

Midland Publishing Limited

Published by
Midland Publishing Limited
24 The Hollow, Earl Shilton
Leicester, LE9 7NA, England
Tel: 01455 847 815   Fax: 01455 841 805
E-mail: midlandbooks@compuserve.com

Design concept and layout
© Midland Publishing Limited and
Stephen Thompson Associates

Edited by Ken Ellis

Printed in England by
MN Productions, Brackmills,
Northampton, Northants

Title Page Illustration:
*The other two elements of the current RAF
fighter/strike 'triad', Harrier GR.7 and the
Jaguar GR.1 – the latter seen here with
overwing AIM-9 Sidewinder missiles.*

CONTENTS

Acknowledgements:
The majority of the photographs come from
the files of Military Aircraft Photographs
(see page 159) with additional contributions
from the following: Patrick Allen, David
Billinge, Austin J Brown, Malcolm Court,
Alan Curry, Ken Ellis, Hugh Harkins,
F Humblot, Morley Lester, Werner
Munzenmaier, John Rogers, John Steptoe,
Bob Sutherland, Pieter Zastrow.

Also to the Army, Royal Air Force and
Royal Navy Public Relations departments;
and to the PR departments of Bell Helicopter
Textron, British Aerospace, Euroflag, GKN-
Westland, Grob, Lockheed Martin, McDon-
nell Douglas Helicopters, Shorts.

Three-view illustrations courtesy Key
Publishing Ltd , others specially commis-
sioned from Pete West.

Additional thanks to Malcolm English of
AIR International and to Alan Warnes and
David Oliver of *AirForces Monthly*.

INTRODUCTION

Following the end of the 'Cold War', the armed forces of NATO and the Warsaw Pact have been changing rapidly as they try to reshape themselves to deal with the new world order. This is an ongoing situation, and one that makes producing a book such as this especially difficult as there is never a point at which the changes come to a halt! As there have been a number of significant changes recently, 1st July 1997 has been set as the dateline for this work .

The first withdrawal from Germany goes ahead in July 1997 with the transfer of 18 Squadron to Odiham from Laarbruch. This is part of the wide-ranging changes to the helicopter force which will result in Odiham becoming an all-Chinook station and Benson will eventually become an all-Merlin base. The final days of the Wessex and Puma will be seen out in Northern Ireland with 72 and 230 Squadrons. In 1996 the combining of the Air Experience Flights into the University Air Squadron (UAS) structure came about and late 1997 should see details emerging of the planned 'civilianisation' of the UASs, with a civilian contractor supplying aircraft to be flown probably by a mix of 'pure' civilian pilots and RAFVR officers under the overall control of an RAF officer.

Within the main body of the book, each section is treated in a similar manner, ie an alphabetic listing of aircraft types, sub divided into broad roles or formats, with details of specification, manufacturer, role and variants, colour scheme details etc. A three-view drawing of the type is also given as an aid to recognition. Particular attention has been paid to the photographs with the view to providing as complete a coverage as possible. While in most cases the illustration will be of a currently serving machine with the unit involved, sometimes a recent example has been used. The exception to this comes with the myriad Volunteer Gliding Schools and the many Army Air Corps Gazelle and Lynx units.

The opportunity to cross-refer and to index is frequently taken, to allow the reader to use the book to the full. (For example, the introductory sections for each of the major armed forces includes an index to units within the command structure and the appendix 'Military Airfields' on page 153 serves as a unit index by location.

In the sections dealing with the aircraft allocated to the units, where an aircraft has departed to St Athan, Fleetlands, civilian contractors, etc for major overhauls or other work we have assumed that they are still with their original user units as in most cases they will return to that unit after the work is complete. Aircraft in long term storage have not been listed as this book is intended to give information on actual *working* units.

There are a number of overseas detachments, particularly for the RAF, these usually result from past or current conflicts and the need to keep assets in those areas. Normally, a number of aircraft or helicopters are allocated to these detachments and they remain in situ while the crews, often from different squadrons, rotate around the aircraft. As the aircraft also rotate on a regular basis back to their home bases when scheduled maintenance is due, we have listed the aircraft under their original units.

No attempt has been made to list stored, derelict or displayed aircraft ('gate guards' and unit 'mascots'). These are well detailed in our own *Wrecks & Relics* and Pocketbook No.2 *Aviation Museums of Britain*.

Within the flying unit information, the type operated is given and the operating base(s). Aircraft sub-types are keyed as shown.

Markings that will help to identify the unit are given plus any other relevant information to help the reader, including further cross referencing.

Aircraft are then listed in serial number order, where no individual code letter is allocated, or in code order where the unit has adopted this system. Where applicable, the code is given first (eg 50:ZD438) because it is the code that will probably be the most obvious form of identity – serial numbers are becoming harder and harder to discern on modern military aircraft!

The serial number currently in operation by the Ministry of Defence started in 1940 with AA100 (a Bristol Blenheim IV), carrying on in sequence to AZ999, to BA100 ((both Blenheim Vs) and so on. Unit recent times, 'holes' in the system (called 'black out blocks) were put in to confuse the enemy and several alphabet groupings were not allocated. The modern day MoD serial system is now sequential without 'holes' with the latest serial numbers (ZJ243 to ZJ280) going to the 'privatised' Squirrels of the DHFS (see page 10) at Shawbury and Middle Wallop. (For a thorough exposition, our *British Military Aircraft Serials 1878-1987* by Bruce Robertson is a must and available from the publishers.) Except in the rarest of cases a serial number stays with the aircraft for the length of its career with the MoD.

Individual aircraft codes are a way of representing an aircraft within a unit (as opposed to an air arm or a country) and frequently take the form of a single-letter (eg 'R') or double-letter ('DN') or a single-digit ('4') or double-digit ('48') displayed prominently on the airframe. There are other systems and these will be readily picked up from following the entries. Unlike serials, codes are frequently changed among aircraft and even units, so be on your mettle!

Note that several aircraft carry their 'last two' (digits) or 'last three' (digits) of their serial number and these appear to be codes but, being an abbreviation of the permanent identity do not 'work' in the same manner.

The continuing move to 'privatisation' has been mentioned already. This means that there are an increasing number of civilian registered aircraft operating in a fundamentally military role within the UK and these have been included in this work. (This is *not* the place to go into the workings of the British civil aircraft register!)

The 'privatisation' mostly comes in two forms: Contractor Owned, Contractor Operated (COCO) is the favoured route, and aircraft can be civilian registered where their work can fit in with the requirements of the Civil Aviation Authority (eg the JEFTS Fireflies, see page 82, or given military serials where they cannot (eg the FOT Dauphins, see page 106). There are also Ministry Owned, Contractor Operated (MOCO) aircraft, which all have military serials. Most well-known of these are the FRADU Hawks, see page 121.

We can confidently expect to find many more references to COCO in the next edition of *Air Forces UK!*

We welcome comments, additions and corrections, please contact us via the publishers at:

Midland Publishing Ltd
24 The Hollow, Earl Shilton,
Leicester, LE9 7NA.

Graeme Pickering & Brian Pickering
Aslackby, Lincs
July 1997

ROYAL AIR FORCE

ROYAL AIR FORCE

Current organisation: numbers after units refer to a page reference within the main text.

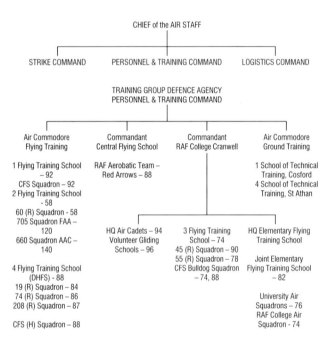

CHIEF of the AIR STAFF

STRIKE COMMAND · PERSONNEL & TRAINING COMMAND · LOGISTICS COMMAND

TRAINING GROUP DEFENCE AGENCY
PERSONNEL & TRAINING COMMAND

Air Commodore Flying Training	Commandant Central Flying School	Commandant RAF College Cranwell	Air Commodore Ground Training

Air Commodore Flying Training

1 Flying Training School – 92
CFS Squadron – 92
2 Flying Training School - 58
60 (R) Squadron - 58
705 Squadron FAA – 120
660 Squadron AAC – 140

4 Flying Training School (DHFS) - 88
19 (R) Squadron – 84
74 (R) Squadron – 86
208 (R) Squadron – 87

CFS (H) Squadron – 88

Commandant Central Flying School

RAF Aerobatic Team – Red Arrows – 88

HQ Air Cadets – 94
Volunteer Gliding Schools – 96

Commandant RAF College Cranwell

3 Flying Training School – 74
45 (R) Squadron – 90
55 (R) Squadron – 78
CFS Bulldog Squadron – 74, 88

Air Commodore Ground Training

1 School of Technical Training, Cosford
4 School of Technical Training, St Athan

HQ Elementary Flying Training School

Joint Elementary Flying Training School – 82

University Air Squadrons – 76
RAF College Air Squadron - 74

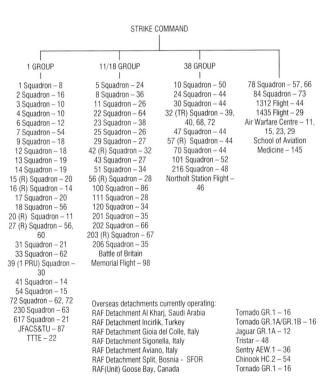

STRIKE COMMAND

1 GROUP	11/18 GROUP	38 GROUP	
1 Squadron – 8	5 Squadron – 24	10 Squadron – 50	78 Squadron – 57, 66
2 Squadron – 16	8 Squadron – 36	24 Squadron – 44	84 Squadron – 73
3 Squadron – 10	11 Squadron – 26	30 Squadron – 44	1312 Flight – 44
4 Squadron – 10	22 Squadron – 64	32 (TR) Squadron – 39,	1435 Flight – 29
6 Squadron – 12	23 Squadron – 38	40, 68, 72	Air Warfare Centre – 11,
7 Squadron – 54	25 Squadron – 26	47 Squadron – 44	15, 23, 29
9 Squadron – 18	29 Squadron – 27	57 (R) Squadron – 44	School of Aviation
12 Squadron – 18	42 (R) Squadron – 32	70 Squadron – 44	Medicine – 145
13 Squadron – 19	43 Squadron – 27	101 Squadron – 52	
14 Squadron – 19	51 Squadron – 34	216 Squadron – 48	
15 (R) Squadron – 20	56 (R) Squadron – 28	Northolt Station Flight –	
16 (R) Squadron – 14	100 Squadron – 86	46	
17 Squadron – 20	111 Squadron – 28		
18 Squadron – 56	120 Squadron – 34		
20 (R) Squadron – 11	201 Squadron – 35		
27 (R) Squadron – 56,	202 Squadron – 66		
60	203 (R) Squadron – 67		
31 Squadron – 21	206 Squadron – 35		
33 Squadron – 62	Battle of Britain		
39 (1 PRU) Squadron –	Memorial Flight – 98		
30			
41 Squadron – 14			
54 Squadron – 15			
72 Squadron – 62, 72			
230 Squadron – 63			
617 Squadron – 21			
JFACS&TU – 87			
TTTE – 22			

Overseas detachments currently operating:
RAF Detachment Al Kharj, Saudi Arabia   Tornado GR.1 – 16
RAF Detachment Incirlik, Turkey   Tornado GR.1A/GR.1B – 16
RAF Detachment Gioia del Colle, Italy   Jaguar GR.1A – 12
RAF Detachment Sigonella, Italy   Tristar – 48
RAF Detachment Aviano, Italy   Sentry AEW.1 – 36
RAF Detachment Split, Bosnia - SFOR   Chinook HC.2 – 54
RAF(Unit) Goose Bay, Canada   Tornado GR.1 – 16

Contractor owned and operated, not in above organisation diagram:
FR Aviation – 80

HARRIER GR.7 and T.10

Specification (GR.7):
Powerplant: One Rolls-Royce Pegasus Mk.105 vectored thrust turbofan of 21,750lb st (96.75kN) dry.
Performance: Maximum speed ('clean') 601mph (967km/h) at 36,000ft (10,972m). Ferry range 2,015 miles (3,242km). Typical combat radius 550 miles (885km).
Weights: Empty 15,542lb (7,050kg). Max take-off 31,000lb (14,061kg).
Dimensions: Span 30ft 4in (9.25m). Length 47ft 1⅛in (14.36m). Height 11ft 7¾in (3.55m).
Armament: Max ordnance 9,200lb (4,173kg) on six wing and one centre-line station. Two fuselage-mounted ADEN 25mm cannon. Provision for bombs, rocket pods, AIM-9 Sidewinder air-to-air missiles. Currently with limited reconnaissance capability.

Manufacturer: British Aerospace/McDonnell Douglas, Warton, Lancs and Dunsfold, Surrey. Production for RAF complete.

Role & Variants: Single-seat vertical/short take-off and landing (V/STOL) air interdiction and close air support fighter (GR.7) and two-seat role-capable conversion trainer (T.10). (USAF designation corresponds to AV-8B and TAV-8B respectively.)

First entered service: 1990 (GR.7).

Notes: With the draw-down from RAF Germany, Cottesmore will become the central Harrier base, with nearby Wittering becoming the maintenance and operational training centre. This should take effect during 1999. The Harrier force now carries 'unique' fleet code numbers to facilitate loans and transfers within the units.

Colour scheme: Along with the Jaguars and Tornado GR.1s, Harriers are currently standardising on an all-over tactical grey colour scheme, although the previous drab green lingers. (Washable white 'snow' camouflage is used for deployments to Norway etc.)

See also: Royal Navy operate the Sea Harrier F/A2 and two-seater variants (see page 102) plus 'Test & Trials' (page 143).

1 Squadron	Harrier GR.7, T.10*	RAF Wittering

Winged '1' mostly carried on fin top, sometimes on the forward jet nozzle cowl. During April 1996 1 Squadron adopted the Harrier fleet number codes, in common with 3, 4 and 20(R) Squadrons – worn in white on the fin.

02:ZD321	03:ZD322	10:ZD329	28:ZD380	30:ZD401	32:ZD403	35:ZD406
45:ZD433	48:ZD436	50:ZD438	51:ZD461	52:ZD462	55:ZD465	58:ZD468
60:ZD470	61:ZG471	92:ZG860	106:ZH658*			

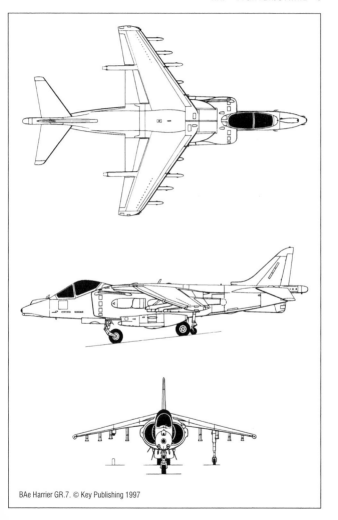

BAe Harrier GR.7. © Key Publishing 1997

3 Squadron   Harrier GR.7, T.10*   RAF Laarbruch

Dragon (cockatrice) on white circle, mostly carried on the forward jet nozzle cowl. Harrier fleet numbers in yellow on fin. Some Laarbruch aircraft unallocated, see under 4 Squadron.

07:ZD326	08:ZD327	09:ZD328	11:ZD330	13:ZD346	23:ZD375	24:ZD376
26:ZD378	27:ZD379	64:ZG474	71:ZG500	74:ZG503	75:ZG504	77:ZG506
78:ZG507	85:ZG531	86:ZG532	104:ZH656*			

4 Squadron   Harrier GR.7, T.10*   RAF Laarbruch

Lightning flash, on the forward jet nozzle cowl and fin tip. Harrier fleet numbers in white on fin.

11:ZD330	15:ZD348	18:ZD351	19:ZD352	47:ZD435	56:ZD466	69:ZG479
79:ZG508	81:ZG510	83:ZG512	84:ZG530	88:ZG856	90:ZG858	91:ZG859
94:ZG862	112:ZH664*					

20 (R) Squadron **Harrier GR.7, T.10*** **RAF Wittering**

An eagle, on the forward jet nozzle cowl. Harrier fleet numbers in white on fin, although most of the T.10s have yet to conform. No.20 (Reserve) Squadron was reformed out 233 Operational Conversion Unit in 1992.

05:ZD324	12:ZD345	14:ZD347	36:ZD407	43:ZD431	46:ZD434	49:ZD437
53:ZD463	54:ZD464	O:ZH659*	P:ZH660*	Q:ZH663*	R:ZH662*	S:ZH665*
Z;ZH661*	XX:ZH657 *					

SAOEU **Harrier GR.7** **DTEO Boscombe Down**

Part of Air Warfare Centre, Strike Attack Operational Evaluation Unit (SAOEU) is a tactics and doctrine unit that also operates Jaguars (p12) and Tornado GR.1s (p16). Tornado and Harrier logo on nose and multi-winged sword carried on fin. Single letter code on extreme fin tip.

E:ZG501	O:ZG472	U:ZD411	ZD467

JAGUAR GR.1 and T.2

Specification (GR.1A):
Powerplant: Two Rolls-Royce/Turboméca Adour Mk.104 turbofans each of 5,320lb st (23.66kN) dry.
Performance: Maximum speed ('clean') 1,056mph (1,699km/h) at 36,000ft (10,972m). Typical combat radius 530 miles (852km).
Weights: Empty 16,975lb (7,700kg). Max take-off 34,612lb (15,700kg).
Dimensions: Span 28ft 6in (8.69m). Length 55ft 2½in (16.83m). Height 16ft ½in (4.89m).
Armament: Max ordnance load 10,000lb (4,536kg) on four wing and one centre-line station capable of taking a wide variety of munitions. Two 30mm ADEN cannon in the lower forward fuselage. Some aircraft have provision for AIM-9L Sidewinder air-to-air missiles on over-wing pylons.

Manufacturer: British Aerospace (previously BAC, as part of the SEPECAT combine with Dassault-Breguet of France), Warton, Lancs. Production complete, upgrades underway.

Role & Variants: Single-seat attack and reconnaissance fighter (GR.1/A) and two-seat role-capable conversion/advanced trainer (T.2/A). Recent upgrades to take TIALD target designator plus further nav/attack avionics updates have led to interim status designated GR.1A(T) and T.2A(T). Aircraft that can take a variety of reconnaissance pods are given a (R) suffix, while others are thought to be suffixed (RT). Interim modifications have produced the GR.1B (plus sub-variants) and these will lead to the even more comprehensive GR.3 and T.4 refits now underway.

First entered service: 1973 (GR.1).

Notes: Coltishall units tend to pool their aircraft. Aircraft have been listed under the squadron to which their codes are allocated. Coltishall Jaguars took over the airspace monitoring task Operation 'Deliberate Guard' in February 1997, based in Italy.

Colour scheme: Jaguars are currently standardising on an all-over tactical grey colour scheme, although the previous grey/green lingers.

See also: 'Test & Trials' (page 143).

6 Squadron   Jaguar GR.1A, GR.1A(T)+, GR.1B±, T.2A*
RAF Coltishall

Winged can-opener carried on air intakes. Two-letter codes beginning 'E' carried in white on the fin. See 'Notes' above.

EC:XZ381+ ED:XZ372± EE:XX737 EF:XZ369± EH:XX970+ EJ:XZ399±
EL:XX729± EM:XZ396 EN:XZ109 EP:XZ356 EQ:XX752 ES:XX841*
ET:XX845* EV:XX141*

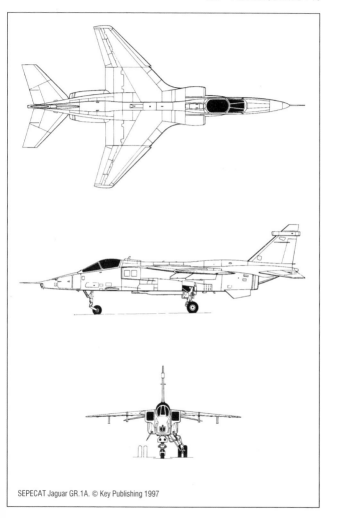

SEPECAT Jaguar GR.1A. © Key Publishing 1997

16 (R) Squadron   Jaguar GR.1A, T.2A*   RAF Lossiemouth

The 'Saint' character (fin) and crossed keys (intake), both on a back circle. Single-letter codes in black on the fin. No.16 (Reserve) Squadron was reformed out of 226 Operational Conversion Unit in 1991.

A:XZ391	B:XZ377	C:XZ385	D:XX745	T:XX139*	U:XX144*
W:XX150*	Y:XX829*	Z:XX832*			

41 Squadron   Jaguar GR.1A, GR.1B(R) + T.2A*, T.2A(T) ±
RAF Coltishall

Cross of Lorraine with red/white stripes on intake, red/white stripes on fin. Two-letter codes beginning 'F' carried in white on the fin. See 'Notes' above, and further illustration below, right.

FA:XZ398	FC:XZ115	FD:XZ113	FF:XZ118	H:XZ107+	FJ:XZ355	FK:XZ357
FM:XZ104	FN:XZ360	FO:XZ363+	P:XZ103	FR:XZ106+	FS:XZ366	T:XZ361
FV:XX842*	FY:XX835±					

54 Squadron **Jaguar GR.1A, GR.1A(T)+, GR.1B§, GR.1B(T)±,**
T.2A*, T.2A(T)= **RAF Coltishall**

Lion on yellow shield with blue/yellow chequers (intake), blue/yellow chequers on fin. Two-letter codes beginning 'G' carried in black on the fin. See 'Notes' above.

GA:XZ112 GB:XX720 GD:XX119± GE:XX767± GG:XX738± GH:XX974
GJ:XZ364± GK:XX748+ GL:XZ108 GN:XZ394 GP:XZ367§ GQ:XX723±
GT:XX146= GU:XX725+ GV:XX846*

SAOEU **Jaguar T.2A** **DTEO Boscombe Down**

Part of Air Warfare Centre, Strike Attack Operational Evaluation Unit (SAOEU) is a tactics and doctrine unit that also operates Harrier GR.7s (page 8) and Tornado GR.1s (page 16). SAOEU uses Jaguar T.2A XX833 'full-time', but recently has also been flying some Coltishall examples, including XX108, as part of the work-up on the GR.3 and T.4 programme.

TORNADO GR.1

Specification (GR.1):
Powerplant: Two Turbo-Union RB.199-34R Mk.103 turbofans each of 8,650lb st (38.48kN) dry.
Performance: Maximum speed ('clean') 921mph (1,482km/h) at 36,000ft (10,972m). Typical combat radius 863 miles (1,390km).
Weights: Empty, approx 30,620lb (13,890kg). Max take-off, approx 61,620lb (27,951kg).
Dimensions: Span 45ft 7½in (13.91m) unswept, 28ft 2½in (8.60m) fully swept. Length 54ft 10¼in (16.72m). Height 19ft 6¼in (5.95m).
Armament: Max ordnance load approx 20,000lb (9,072kg) on four wing and two under fuselage stations. Two 27mm IWKA-Mauser cannon in the forward fuselage. Large range of bombs, designator and chaff pods, anti-radiation missiles, Sea Eagle anti-ship missiles (GR.1B) etc. Two AIM-9L Sidewinders on inner wing pylons.

Manufacturer: Panavia (a combination of British Aerospace, DASA Germany and Alenia, Italy in their present forms), Warton, Lancs. Production for the RAF completed, upgrades to GR.4 and GR.4A underway.

Role & Variants: Two-seat all-weather variable-geometry strike/attack (GR.1, GR.4A), battlefield reconnaissance (GR.1A) and maritime strike (GR.1B) aircraft. GR.1(T) fully role-capable conversion trainer, but use of the designation appears to have lapsed. Details of GR.4 and GR.4A on page 23

First entered service: 1980 with TTTE, 1982 with 9 Squadron (both GR.1).

Notes: Eventual bases and/or fates for the German-based units have yet to be announced. Intended codes are shown in brackets. The Tornado force maintains a detachment at Goose Bay, Canada, for training purposes.

Colour scheme: Along with the Harriers and Jaguars, Tornado GR.1s are currently standardising on an all-over tactical grey colour scheme, although the grey and green lingers.

Sea also: The Air Defence Variant (ADV), Tornado F.3 (see page 24) and 'Test & Trials' (page 143).

---

2 Squadron **Tornado GR.1, GR.1A*** **RAF Marham**
Rope knot on white circle with white triangles on black background on forward nose and fin tip. Single-letter codes/Roman numerals in black on white triangle on fin. Detachment maintained at Incirlik, Turkey, on Operation 'Warden'. See 'Notes' above.

A:ZA370	E:ZA372	H:ZA373	I:ZD996	N:ZA395	R:ZA401	S:ZA398
T:ZA400	W:ZA404	Y:ZA405	II:ZA367*	IV:ZA551*		

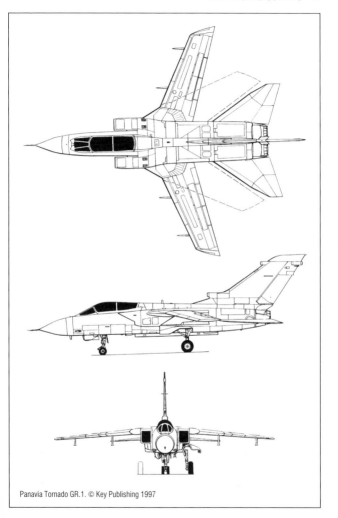

Panavia Tornado GR.1. © Key Publishing 1997

9 Squadron   Tornado GR.1   RAF Brüggen, Germany

Green bat on tail, green arrowhead around roundel. Two-letter codes beginning 'A' on fin. Note that all of the Brüggen squadrons have aircraft on detachment for Operation 'Jural' in Saudi Arabia.

AB:ZD746	AC:ZD739	AE:ZD890	AG:ZD720	AJ:ZD851	AK:ZD748	AL:ZD747
AP:ZD714	AX:ZG756	AY:ZG769				

12 Squadron   Tornado GR.1*, GR.1B   RAF Lossiemouth

Fox's head on fin tip. Two-letter codes beginning 'F' on fin.

FA:ZA447	FB:ZA450	FC:ZA452	FD:ZA453	FE:ZA455	FF:ZA474	FG:ZA473
FH:ZA475	FJ:ZA490	FK:ZA491	FL:ZA492	FQ:ZA409	(FT):ZA365*	
FX:ZA599*	FZ:ZA410*					

13 Squadron　　　　　**Tornado GR.1*, GR.1A**　　　　　**RAF Marham**

Face of a lynx plus sword on shield, with blue/yellow stripe on fin tip, lightning flashes on blue and green background flanking nose roundel. Single-letter codes, plus the lone GR.1 with Roman numeral in black on fin. See 'Notes' above.

B:ZG707　　F:ZG712　　G:ZG713　　J:ZG705　　K:ZG726　　L:ZG727　　M:ZG729
P:ZG711　　V:ZG709　　XIII:ZG752*

14 Squadron　　　　　**Tornado GR.1**　　　　　**RAF Brüggen, Germany**

Red cross on white disc topped by wings, flanked by blue diamonds on white background (on nose), blue diamonds on fin tip. Two-letter codes beginning 'B' on fin. Note that all of the Brüggen squadrons have aircraft on detachment for Operation 'Jural' in Saudi Arabia.

BA:ZD809　　BB:ZD790　　BC:ZD811　　BD:ZD744　　BE:ZA393　　BF:ZD895
BG:ZD749　　BJ:ZD892　　BK:ZD707　　BM:ZD745　　BP:ZG794　　BQ:ZA470
BS:ZG777　　BT:ZD849　　BW:ZD812　　BY:ZD712

15 (R) Squadron   Tornado GR.1   RAF Lossiemouth

'XV' in white on fin tip. Two-letter codes beginning 'T' on fin. The former Tornado Weapons Conversion Unit and will absorb the RAF element of the TTTE in April 1999 (see page 22).

TA:ZA597	TB:ZA614	TC:ZA563	TD:ZA587	TE:ZA589	TG:ZA560	TF:ZA556
TH:ZA600	TI:ZA601	TJ:ZA607	TK:ZA608	TL:ZA613	TM:ZA558	TO:ZA541
TP:ZA544	TQ:ZA548	TR:ZA549	TS:ZA552	TT:ZA562	TU:ZA594	TV:ZA595
TW:ZD713	TX:ZA602	TY:ZA604	TZ:ZA612	ZA559 is named *MacRobert's Reply*.		

17 Squadron   Tornado GR.1   RAF Brüggen, Germany

Red gauntlet on black/white shield on fin. Two-letter codes beginning 'C' on fin. Note that all of the Brüggen squadrons have aircraft on detachment for Operation 'Jural' in Saudi Arabia.

CA:ZD793	CB:ZD788	CC:ZD715	CD:ZD848	CE:ZA458	CF:ZD792
CG:ZA462	CH:ZD847	CI:ZA406	CJ:ZD843	CK:ZA564	CR:ZA463	CT:ZA472
CX:ZD743	CY:ZD741	CZ:ZD742			

31 Squadron   **Tornado GR.1**   **RAF Brüggen, Germany**

Yellow star on fin, yellow and green arrow head around fuselage roundel. Two-letter codes beginning 'D' on fin. Note that all of the Brüggen squadrons have aircraft on detachment for Operation 'Jural' in Saudi Arabia.

DA:ZD740	DB:ZD810	DC:ZG791	DD:ZG792	DE:ZD719	DG:ZD709
DK:ZG779	DN:ZG775	DR:ZD850	DW:ZG771	DX:ZD842	DY:ZD711

617 Squadron   **Tornado GR.1*, GR.1B**   **RAF Lossiemouth**

Red lightning flashes on black background flanking nose roundel, red flash on back background on fin tip. Three-letter codes, all beginning 'AJ' on fin tip. Detachment maintained at Incirlik, Turkey, on Operation 'Warden'.

A:ZA460	B:ZA459	C:ZA399	F:ZA465	G:ZA407	J:ZA457	(K):ZA471
L:ZA374	M:ZA461	O:ZA469	Q:ZA456	S:ZA411	T:ZA598 *	W:ZA375

TTTE Tornado GR.1 RAF Cottesmore

(Tornado Tri-National Tornado Training Establishment) 'TTTE' in white within black dart on the fin. Two-digit 'unique' code prefixed with 'B-' (Britain), 'G-' (Germany) or 'I-' (Italy) on the fin. This unit trains Tornado crews for the air forces of Germany, Italy and the UK, with each country providing aircraft and instructors for that purpose and taking it in turns to command the unit. Establishment is four squadrons, 'A', 'B' and 'C' undertaking conversion training and 'S' overseeing standards. Over the next two years the unit will gradually wind down, with the base being vacated completely by December 1999 when it will be the home of the RAF's Harrier force (see page 8). German Tornado training will be transferred to their new detachment at Holloman Air Force Base, New Mexico, USA and the Italian detachment will also be withdrawn. The remaining RAF aircraft will move to Lossiemouth, officially on 1st April 1999 and become part of 15 (R) Squadron there, see page 20.

RAF

B-01:ZA320	B-02:ZA324	B-03:ZA325	B-04:ZA352	B-05:ZA357	B-07:ZA356
B-08:ZA330	B-09:ZA362	B-11:ZA319	B-14:ZA323	B-50:ZA322	B-54:ZA355
B-56:ZA360	B-57:ZA361	B-58:ZA321			

German Air Force

G-20:43+01	G-21:43+02	G-22:43+03	G-24:43+05	G-25:43+06	G-26:43+07
G-28:43+09	G-29:43+10	G-30:43+11	G-31:43+15	G-32:43+16	G-33:43+17
G-39:43+42	G-71:43+13	G-72:43+14	G-73:43+32	G-75:43+25	G-77:43+75

Italian Air Force

I-40:MM55001	I-41:MM55002	I-42:MM55000
I-43:MM55003	I-93:MM7003	

SAOEU   Tornado GR.1, GR.1A*/B+   DTEO Boscombe Down

Part of Air Warfare Centre, Strike Attack Operational Evaluation Unit (SAOEU) is a tactics and doctrine unit that also operates Harriers (page 8) and Jaguars (page 12). Tornado and Harrier logo on nose and multi-winged sword carried on fin. Single letter code on extreme fin tip.
E:ZG706*   O:ZD716   U:ZA446+

Tornado GR.4

In May 1993 British Aerospace first flew development Tornado GR.1 P.15 (XZ631) in its new guise as the GR.4 'demonstrator'. The GR.4/GR.4A mid-life update programme has suffered from delays and budget constraints, but the first 'full' GR.4 conversion (ZG750) made its first flight from Warton on 4th April 1997. Major recognition features for the GR.4 include the additional under nose fairing containing a forward-looking infra-red sensor. Among the equipment installed in the upgrade are night vision goggles, global positioning system, and enhanced avionics and computer systems. Conversions are due for delivery to operational units in 1998.

TORNADO F.3

Specification (F.3):

Powerplant: Two Turbo-Union RB.199-34R Mk.104 turbofans each of 9,100lb st (40.48kN) dry.

Performance: Maximum speed ('clean') 1,453mph (2,338km/h) at 36,000ft (10,972m). Ferry range approx 2,420 miles (3,90km). Typical combat radius approx 1,000 miles (1,151km) subsonic.

Weights: Empty, approx 31,970lb (14,502kg). Max take-off, approx 61,700lb (27,986kg).

Dimensions: Span 45ft 7½in (13.91m) unswept, 28ft 2½in (8.60m) fully swept. Length 61ft 3½in (18.68m). Height 19ft 6¼in (5.95m).

Armament: Four BAe Skyflash air-to-air missiles mounted semi-recessed in the under fuselage, up to four AIM-9L Sidewinder air-to-air-missiles on two wing pylons. One 27mm IWKA-Mauser cannon in the forward fuselage.

Manufacturer: Panavia (a combination of British Aerospace, DASA Germany and Alenia, Italy in their present forms), Warton, Lancs. Production for the RAF completed.

Role & Variants: Two-seat all-weather variable-geometry long range interceptor. A fully role-capable conversion and continuation trainer version is the F.3(T), but use of the designation appears to have lapsed. (Prior to the F.3, a development batch of 18 aircraft, designated F.2s were used for operational evaluation, the bulk are in store and/or in use for an F.3 repair programme. See 'Test & Trials' on page 143 for the 'operational' F.2s.)

First entered service: 1986 (F.3).

Notes: BAe Warton is currently engaged in a repair process to some F.3s which involves the grafting on of the centre section of F.2s held in deep store at St Athan, South Wales. Aircraft involved are as follows: ZE154, ZE251, ZE254, ZE255, ZE258, ZE288, ZE292, ZE294, ZE295, ZE343, ZE728, ZE729, ZE736, ZE759, ZE786, ZE793. The Italian Air Force is leasing 24 RAF F.3s as stop-gaps until the arrival of the Eurofighter EF 2000.

Colour scheme: All wear an all-over air defence grey.

See also: Tornado GR.1/GR.4 (see page 16) and 'Test & Trials' (page 143).

5 Squadron   **Tornado F.3**   **RAF Coningsby**

Green maple leaf flanked by red bands on fin, red arrowhead around fuselage roundel. Two-letter codes beginning 'C' in white on the fin.

CA:ZG757	CB:ZG795	CC:ZG730	CC:ZG770	CE:ZG796	(CF):ZE729
(CH):ZE758	CO:ZG772	CT:ZE830	CV:ZH555	CY:ZG793	

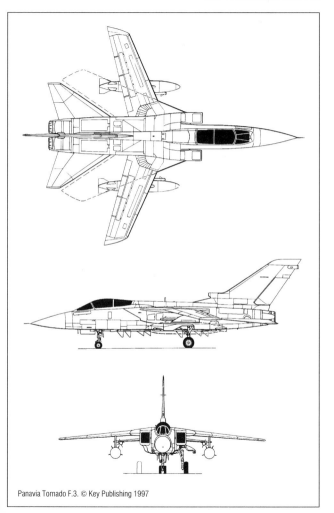

Panavia Tornado F.3. © Key Publishing 1997

11 Squadron   Tornado F.3   RAF Leeming

Two eagles in flight in black on the fin. Yellow triangles with black background flanking the fuselage roundel. Two-letter codes beginning 'D' in black on the fin. (* ZE968 wears the special code 'DXI'.)

DA:ZE164	DB:ZE200	DC:ZE158	DD:ZE204	(DF):ZE788	DG:ZE763	DH:ZE764
(DI):ZE969	DJ:ZE887	(DK):ZE942	DL:ZE936	DM:ZE968*	DN:ZE983	DO:ZE201
DV:ZE160	DW:ZE965	(DY):ZE964	DZ:ZE966		

25 Squadron   Tornado F.3   RAF Leeming

Hawk and a gauntletted hand, in black on fin. Two-letter codes beginning 'F' in white on the fin. ZE165 has the special code 'ZK' for the 1997 display season.

FA:ZE808	FD:ZE961	FF:ZE737	FG:ZE161	FI:ZE203	FJ:ZE962	FK:ZE162
FL:ZE199	(FM):ZE907	(FN):ZE168	(FO):ZE165	FU:ZE967	FV:ZE888	

29 Squadron　　　Tornado F.3　　　RAF Coningsby

Eagle in flight attacking a buzzard, both in black on the fin. Two-letter codes beginning 'B' on the fin.

BA:ZE785	BB:ZE732	(BC):ZE295	BD:ZG770	BE:ZE341	BF:ZG797
BG:ZG778	BJ:ZG755	BK:ZE339	BL:ZG731	BX:ZE256	BY:ZE157

43 Squadron　　　Tornado F.3　　　RAF Leuchars

Fighting cock on the fin, black and white chequers flanking the fuselage roundel. Two-letter code beginning 'G' in white on fin.

(GA):ZE251	GB:ZE734	GC:ZE207	(GD):ZE790	(GE):ZE963	GF:ZE731
(GG):ZE831	(GI):ZE941	GJ:ZE755	(GK):ZE757	(GL):ZE206	(GQ):ZE291
GR:ZE296					

56 (R) Squadron   Tornado F.3   RAF Coningsby

Multi-coloured phoenix in flames on the fin. Red and white chequers flanking fuselage roundel. Two-letter codes beginning 'A' in white on fin. Undertaking the role of F.3 Operational Conversion Unit, also training Italian Tornado F.3 crews (see 'Notes' above).

(AB):ZH553   AC:ZE253   AD:ZE290   AE:ZE340   AF:ZH557   AG:ZE786   (AI):ZE793
AJ:ZH559   AK:ZH556   AL:ZE735   AN:ZE154   (AO):ZH554   AP:ZE209   (AQ):ZE258
AR:ZE839   AS:ZG776   (AT):ZE288   (AV):ZE794   (AW):ZE254   AX:ZE736   AY:ZE255
(AZ):ZE292

111 Squadron   Tornado F.3   RAF Leuchars

Cross of Palestine in yellow against black circle and bar on fin. Black lightning flash through fuselage roundel. Two-letter codes beginning 'H' in white on fin.

HE:ZE156   HF:ZE289   HG:ZE338   HM:ZE294   HN:ZE257   (HR):ZE159   HS:ZE934
HT:ZE293   HV:ZE908   (HW):ZE342   (HX):ZE728   HY:ZE791

1435 Flight   **Tornado F.3**   **Mount Pleasant Int Airport, Falkland Islands**

Maltese cross on the fin, Falkland Islands badge on the nose. Individual letter codes on the fin relate to the names of the unit's Gloster Gladiators during the defence of Malta – 'F' - *Faith*, 'H' - *Hope*, 'C' - *Charity* and 'D' - *Desperation*.
C:ZG751   D:ZG799   F:ZG798   H:ZG834

F.3 OEU   **Tornado F.3**   **RAF Coningsby**

Part of the Air Warfare Centre (AWC), the F.3 Operational Evaluation Unit is a tactics and doctrine unit. Multi-winged sword of the AWC carried on the fin.
ZE756   SB:ZE889   ZE982   ZH552

CANBERRA T.4, PR.7 and PR.9

Specification (PR.9):
Powerplant: Two Rolls-Royce RA.29 Avon Mk.206 turbojets each of 11,250lb st (50.04kN).
Performance: Maximum speed approx 620mph (997km/h) at 50,000ft 15,240m). Max range 4,500 miles (7,241km).
Weights: Max take-off 57,500lb (26,082kg).
Dimensions: Span 67ft 10in (20.45m). Length 66ft 8in (20.31m). Height 15ft 7in (4.72m).

Manufacturer: Designed and developed by English Electric (now British Aerospace) at Samlesbury and Warton, Lancs; the surviving T.4s and PR.7s built there. PR.9 by Shorts at Sydenham, Northern Ireland. Production completed.

Roles & Variants: Two-seat long range reconnaissance aircraft (PR.7 and PR.9), two-seat conversion trainer (T.4). PR.7s used primarily for chaff-laying training exercises.

First entered service: 1954 (T.4 and PR.7), 1960 (PR.9).

Notes: Under Operation 'Hamden', 39 Squadron PR.9s are tasked with reconnaissance of the states of the former Yugoslavia. Additional commitments for various governments and agencies see the PR.9s on wide-ranging temporary detachments.

Colour scheme: T.4s and PR.7s dark green and dark sea grey camouflage with light aircraft grey undersides. PR.9s hemp upper surfaces with light aircraft grey undersides.

See also: 'Test & Trials' (page 143).

39 (No.1 PRU) Sqn   Canberra T.4+, PR.7*, PR.9   RAF Marham
Winged bomb in black within circle on fin. Two-letter codes beginning 'A' on fin for T.4s and PR.9s, two-letter codes beginning 'B' for PR.7s.
AA:XH131   AB:XH134   AC:XH135   AD:XH168   (AE):XH169   AS:WJ874+
AV:WJ866+   BP:WH779*   BR:WT509*

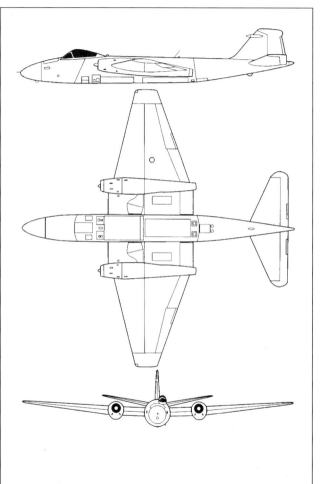

English Electric Canberra PR.9. Pete West © Midland Publishing 1997

NIMROD R.1 AND MR.2

Specification (MR.2):
Powerplant: Four Rolls-Royce RB.168-20 Spey Mk.250 turbojet each of 12,140lb st (53.99kN).
Performance: Max speed 575mph (926km/h). Typical patrol speed 230mph (370km/h). Ferry range 5,758 miles (9,266km). Typical endurance 12-15 hours.
Weights: Empty 86,000lb (39,010kg). Max take-off 177,500lb (80,514kg).
Dimensions: Span 114ft 10in (35.00m). Length 126ft 9in (38.63m). Height 29ft 8⅛in (9.08m).
Armament: Max ordnance 13,500lb (6,124kg). Wide range of sonobuoys, depth charges and bombs, also Stingray torpedoes all within the fuselage weapons bay. Two underwing pylons capable of taking free fall bombs, Harpoon anti-ship missiles, AIM-9 Sidewinder air-to-air missiles for self-defence. Some aircraft modified to accept forward-looking infra-red sensor, electronic countermeasure pods and towed radar decoys.

Manufacturer: Hawker Siddeley (now British Aerospace), Woodford, Manchester. Production completed. MR.4 upgrade underway – see below.

Roles & Variants: Electronic intelligence gathering (R.1) with crews of up to 28; and long range maritime reconnaissance and anti-submarine warfare (MR.2) aircraft. (R.1 not equipped with the magnetic anomaly detector boom at rear of fuselage.)

First entered service: 1969 (MR.1), 1974 (R.1), 1979 (MR.2).

Notes: The British Aerospace led 'Nimrod 2000' (MR.4) 'second generation' upgrade is currently in its prototype phase with the first three airframes at Bournemouth, Dorset, for initial work, fitting out will take place at Warton, Lancs. For more details see under 'The Future' (page 148). No.42 (R), 120, 201 and 206 Squadrons form the Kinloss Wing with pooled Nimrod MR.2s. The Nimrod MR.2 fleet is listed under No.206 Squadron on page 35 with known 'affiliations' marked.

Colour scheme: Hemp upper surfaces and light aircraft grey under surfaces.

42 (R) Squadron   Nimrod MR.2   RAF Kinloss

Figure of Perseus against a globe on the fin fillet. 'Last two' of the serial number in white on the fin. No.42 is the Nimrod MR.2 Operational Conversion squadron and draws aircraft from the Nimrod pool at Kinloss. See 'Notes' and under 206 Squadron.

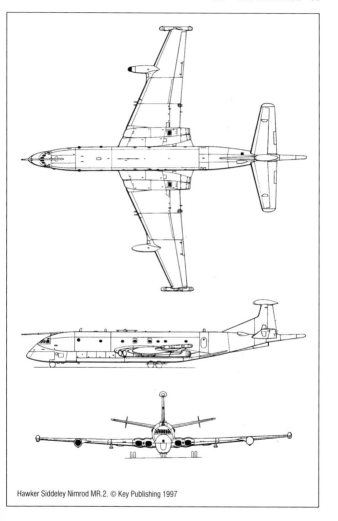

Hawker Siddeley Nimrod MR.2. © Key Publishing 1997

51 Squadron   Nimrod R.1   RAF Waddington
Goose in flight on a white circle on the fin fillet. MR.2 XV249* was ferried from Woodford to
Waddington during December 1996 for installation of the electronics equipment and may
adopt R.1 designation although it is believed not to be a 'full' version.
XV249*   XW664   XW665

120 Squadron   Nimrod MR.2   RAF Kinloss
In general, no special markings, some aircraft carry the squadron number is Roman numerals
('CXX') on the fin. 'Last two' of the serial number in white on the fin. See 'Notes' and under 206
Squadron.

201 Squadron   Nimrod MR.2   RAF Kinloss

In general, no special markings, some aircraft carry the squadron emblem, a seagull, in flight on the fin. 'Last two' of the serial in white on the fin. See 'Notes' and under 206 Squadron.

206 Squadron   Nimrod MR.2   RAF Kinloss

In general, no special markings, some aircraft carry the squadron emblem, an octopus, on the fin. 'Last two' of the serial number in white on the fin. The Kinloss Wing Nimrod MR.2s are as follows, few carry unit markings, those that currently do are marked 42*, 120+, 201=, 206§.

XV226	XV227+	XV228	XV229*	XV230	XV231	XV232
XV233	XV235*	XV236	XV240*	XV241+	XV243§	XV244
XV245=	XV246=	XV248	XV250	XV251	XV252	XV254=
XV255	XV258	XV260	XZ284+			

SENTRY AEW.1

Specification:
Powerplant: Four CFM International CFM56-2A-3 turbofans each of 24,000lb st (106.75kN).
Performance: Max speed 530mph (853km/h) at 36,000ft (10,972m). Typical operating radius 1,150 miles (1,850km). Endurance 11-12 hours (without refuelling).
Weights: 171,950lb (77,996kg). Max take-off 325,000lb (147,420kg).
Dimensions: Span 145ft 9in (44.42m). Length 152ft 11in (46.61m). Height 41ft 9in (12.73m). Rotodome diameter 30ft 0in (9.14m), mounted on 11ft 0in (3.35m) supports.

Manufacturer: Boeing Defense and Space Group, Seattle, Washington, USA.

Role and Variants: Airborne early warning and control (AWACS) platform, 17 crew including 13 mission operatives. (USAF designation E-3D.)

First entered service: 1991.

Notes: With effect from 1st April 1996 the Sentry fleet became jointly operated by 8 and 23 Squadron – having been solely operated by No.8 prior to that. The aircraft carry joint markings, with 8 Squadron to one side and 23 on the other. The Sentry force maintains a detachment at Aviano, Italy, in support of Operation 'Deliberate Guard' over the former Yugoslavia. All seven aircraft carry a picture of one of the 'Seven Dwarfs' from the Walt Disney cartoon film inside the rear of the aircraft. They are ZH101 *Doc*, ZH102 *Dopey*, ZH103 *Happy*, ZH104 *Sleepy*, ZH105 *Sneezy*, ZH106 *Grumpy* and ZH107 *Bashful*.

Colour scheme: All-over air defence grey.

8 Squadron	Sentry AEW.1	RAF Waddington

Arabian dagger on the fin, yellow blue and red bars flanking the fuselage roundel. 'Last two' of the serial number in white on the fin. See 'Notes' above.

ZH101	ZH102	ZH103	ZH104	ZH105	ZH106	ZH107

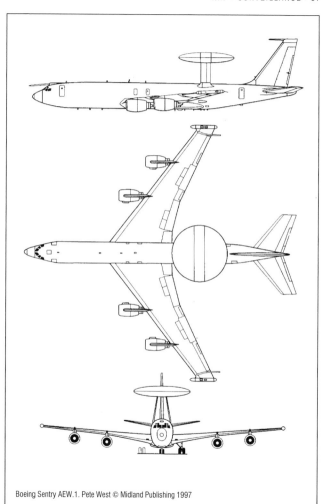

Boeing Sentry AEW.1. Pete West © Midland Publishing 1997

23 Squadron   **Sentry AEW.1**   **RAF Waddington**

Eagle alighting on the fin, red and blue bars flanking the fuselage roundel. 'Last two' of the serial number in white on the fin. See 'Notes' above. Serial numbers as given under 8 Squadron on page 36.

Interior of an 8/23 Squadron Sentry AEW.1.

HS.125 CC.2 and CC.3

Specification (CC.3):

Powerplant: Two Garrett TFE731-5R-1H turbofans each of 4,300lb st (19.26kN).

Performance: Max speed 368mph (592km/h) at sea level. Max range with max payload plus reserves 2,785 miles (4,482km).

Weights: Empty 12,845lb (5,826kg). Max take-off 25,500lb (11,566kg).

Dimensions: Span 47ft 0in (14.33m). Length 50ft 8½in (15.46m). Height 17ft 7in (5.36m).

Accommodation: Five to six passengers, plus steward. Two aircrew. Northrop MIRTS infra-red countermeasures pod in rear fuselage.

Manufacturer: British Aerospace (was Hawker Siddeley), Hawarden, North Wales. Production of series completed, design rights now owned by Raytheon and produced in the USA.

Roles & Variants: Medium range VIP transport. CC.2 corresponds to civilian -600B but re-engined with Garrett TFE731 turbofans; CC.3 to civilian -700B.

First entered service: 1973 (CC.2), 1982 (CC.3).

Notes: No.32 (The Royal) Squadron is essentially an RAF unit, but does include some Fleet Air Arm pilots as the HS.125s are also tasked for VIP work for the Royal Navy. No.32 Squadron also operates the following types: BAe 146 (page 40), Squirrel (page 68), Wessex (page 70).

Colour scheme: Low visibility 'barley' overall with pale blue cheatline, or white overall with dark blue cheatline and all-red tail surfaces.

See also: Dominie T.1 (page 78) navigation trainer based upon early series HS.125 (and for essentially similar general arrangement illustration) plus 'Test & Trials' (page 143).

---

32 (Royal) Sqn   HS.125 CC.2*, CC.3   RAF Northolt

Squadron badge, a hunting horn, carried near the main door on some aircraft. See 'Notes' above. The unit also operates BAe 146s (page 40), Twin Squirrels (page 68) and Wessex HCC.4s (page 70).

XX507*	XX508*	ZD620	ZD621	ZD703	ZD704	ZE395
ZE396						

BAe 146 CC.2

Specification:

Powerplant: Four Textron Lycoming ALF 502R-5 turbofans each of 6,970lb st (31.0kN).

Performance: Max speed 339mph (546km/h). Range with standard fuel and reserves 1,698 miles (2,733km).

Weights: Empty 51,294lb (23,266kg). Max take-off 93,000lb (42,184kg).

Dimensions: 86ft 0in (26.21m). Length 93ft 10in (28.60m). Height 28ft 2in (8.59m).

Accommodation: Can vary but around 20 people typically. Baggage and underfloor holds approx 645ft³ (18.3m³). Loral Matador infra-red jamming system on rear fuselage.

Manufacturer: British Aerospace (now Avro International Aerospace), Hatfield, Herts. BAe 146 production completed. A completely updated version, the RJ, continues in production by Avro at Woodford, Manchester.

Role & Variants: Medium range VIP transport. Corresponds to civilian -200 Statesman variant.

First entered service: 1986.

Colour scheme: White overall with dark blue cheatline and all-red tail surfaces.

32 (The Royal) Squadron   BAe 146 CC.2   RAF Northolt

The unit also operates BAe HS.125s (page 39), Twin Squirrels (page 68) and Wessex HCC.4s (page 70).

ZE700   ZE701   ZE702

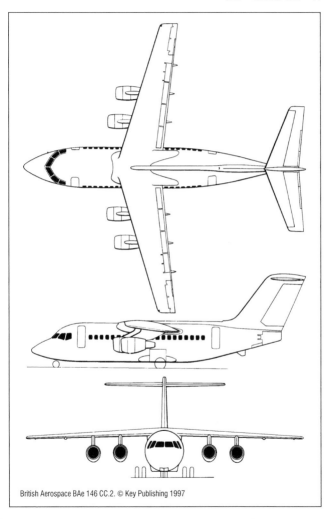

British Aerospace BAe 146 CC.2. © Key Publishing 1997

HERCULES C.1 and C.3

Specification (C.1):
Powerplant: Four Allison T56-A-15 turboprops each of 4,910shp (3,662kW).
Performance: Maximum speed 368mph (592km/h). Range with max payload 2,430 miles (3,910km).
Weights: Empty 69,300lb (31,343kg). Max take-off 155,000lb (70,308kg).
Dimensions: Span 132ft 7¼in (40.41m). Length 98ft 9in (30.09m). Height 38ft 3⅛in (11.65m).
Accommodation: Typically 92 troops, 64 paratroops, 74 casualty stretchers plus two attendants. Maximum payload around 43,000lb (19,504kg). Five aircrew.

Manufacturer: Lockheed Aircraft Corporation, Marietta, Georgia, USA. C-130K production complete, C-130H and 'new generation' C-130J C.4 (see page 45) underway.

Roles & Variants: Medium range tactical transport. C.1 (USAF designation C-130K, essentially similar to the C-130H) with 'standard' fuselage. C.3 (USAF designation C-130K, essentially similar to the C-130H-30) with 15ft 0in (4.57m) fuselage stretch.

First entered service: 1967 (C.1), 1981 (C.3).

Notes: Five remaining stop-gap C.1K in flight refuelling tankers are in storage at Cambridge, Cambs, pending disposal. Lockheed will be taking Hercules C.1/C.3s in trade-in one-for-one with deliveries of Hercules C.4 (and C.5s) as they occur (see page 45).

Colour scheme: Fleet adopting overall medium grey colours, but the dark green/dark grey overall camouflage remains in the majority at present.

See also: 'Test & Trials' page 143. The USAF also operates the C-130 Hercules in the UK, see page 150. See also header illustration on page 5.

Hercules C.1

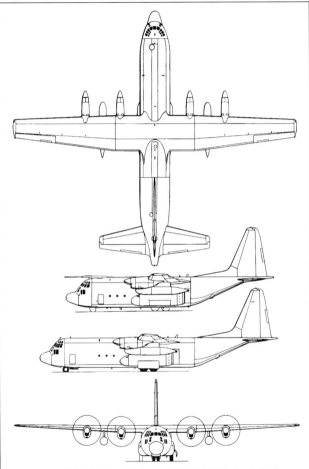

Lockheed Hercules C.3, with additional side view of a C.1. Note that all of the Hercules fleet is now IFR probe equipped.© Key Publishing 1997

Lyneham Transport Wing   Hercules C.1, C.3+   RAF Lyneham
24 Squadron
30 Squadron
47 Squadron
57 (R) Squadron
70 Squadron

These units form the Lyneham Transport Wing of pooled Hercules C.1s and C.3s – see below. No.57 is the Hercules Operational Conversion Unit and will be the first recipient of the Hercules C.4 – see page 45. Apart from occasional special markings, no squadron identities are worn. 'Last three' of the aircraft serial number appears on the nose and the fin, in white on green/grey examples and in black on all-grey machines. See 1312 Flight below.

XV176+	XV177+	XV178	XV179	XV181	XV182	XV183+
XV184+	XV185	XV186	XV187	XV188+	XV189+	XV190+
XV191	XV192	XV195	XV196	XV197+	XV199+	XV200
XV202+	XV205	XV206	XV207+	XV209+	XV210	XV211
XV212+	XV214+	XV215	XV217+	XV218	XV219+	XV220+
XV221+	XV222+	XV223+	XV290+	XV291	XV292	XV293
XV294+	XV295	XV297	XV298	XV299+	XV300	XV301+
XV302+	XV303+	XV304+	XV305+	XV306	XV307+	

1312 Flight   Hercules C.1   Mount Pleasant Int Airport, Falkland Islands

The Flight operates a Hercules C.1 in the maritime reconnaissance role on detachment from the Lyneham Transport Wing (see above) and a VC-10 K.4 (see page 50).

Hercules C.3

HERCULES C.4

Specification (C.4):

Powerplant: Four Allison AE2100D3 turboprops each of 4,591shp (3,424kW) driving six-bladed Dowty R391 propellers.

Performance: Max speed 400mph (645km/h). Range with max payload 3,262 miles (5,250km).

Weights: Empty 79,291lb (35,966kg). Max take-off 155,000lb (70,305kg).

Dimensions: Span 132ft 7¼in (40.41m). Length 113ft 9in (34.66m). Height 38ft 3½in (11.65m).

Accommodation: Typically 128 troops. Max payload around 38,061lb (17,264kg). Three aircrew.

Manufacturer: Lockheed Aeronautical Systems, Marietta, Georgia, USA. Production underway.

Roles & Variants: Medium range tactical transport. C.4 (USAF designation C-130J-30 and known as the Hercules II) with 'stretched' fuselage. Should RAF opt for the 'short' fuselage C-130J, this will be known as the C.5. The C-130J is a 'new generation' Hercules while the airframe is simplified, it is essentially the same.

First entered service: Scheduled for late 1997, but this may slip into 1998.

Notes: As part of the replacement of the Hercules fleet, the RAF placed an order for 25 C-130Js in December 1995, with initially 15 C-130J-30s (ZH865 to ZH879) being ordered, the remainder possibly to be the standard-length C-130J (serials ZH880 to ZH889). (At the same time it was announced that up to 50 Airbus Military Aircraft FLAs (see 'The Future', page 148) would also be ordered. The prototype C-130J-30 (N130JA, ZH865 for the RAF and illustrated below) made its first flight on 5th April 1996. Developmental problems have delayed the anticipated arrived of the first aircraft for acceptance trials at Boscombe Down, Wilts, from the early summer of 1997 to the end of the year at the earliest.

Colour scheme: Overall medium grey.

ISLANDER CC.2 AND CC.2A

Specification:

Powerplant: Two Allison 250-B17C turboprops each of 320shp (238.5kW).

Performance: Max speed 196mph (315km/h). Range 838 miles (1,349km).

Weights: Empty 4,220lb (1,914kg). Max take-off 7,000lb (3,175kg).

Dimensions: Span 49ft 0in (14.94m). Length 35ft 7¾in (10.86m). Height 13ft 8¾in (4.18m).

Manufacturer: Airframe manufacture by IAv Bucharesti in Romania under licence to Pilatus Britten-Norman Ltd, Bembridge, Isle of Wight, who complete to customer requirements.

Roles & Variants: Light transport and special duties aircraft with capability for specialised surveillance work. CC.2A has 'plumbing' for two underwing hard points. (Manufacturer's designation BN-2T Turbine Defender.)

First entered service: 1991.

Colour scheme: Low visibility 'barley' overall with pale blue cheatline.

See also: Islander AL.1 (page 141) and 'Test & Trials' (page 143).

Northolt Station Flight   **Islander CC.2, CC.2A***

RAF Northolt

ZF573*   ZH536

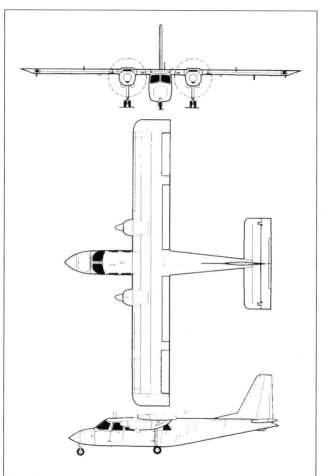

Pilatus Britten-Norman Islander CC.2. Note that the Islander AL.1 is essentially similar, see page 141. Pete West © Midland Publishing 1997

TRISTAR K.1, KC.1, C.2, C.2A

Specification (K.1):

Powerplant: Three Rolls-Royce RB211-524B4 turbofans each of 50,000lb st (222.41kN).

Performance: Max speed 599mph (964km/h). Range with max payload 4,836 miles (7,783km).

Weights: Empty 242,684lb (110,163kg). Max take-off 540,000lb (244,944kg).

Dimensions: Span 164ft 4in (50.09m). Length 164ft 2½in (50.05m). Height 55ft 4in (16.86m).

Accommodation/Payload: K.1: 100,060lb (45,387kg) of transfer fuel available, seating available for up to 100 passenger. KC.1: fitted with 104in x 140in (2.64m x 3.56m) side cargo door with strengthened floor and cargo handling system.

Manufacturer: Lockheed Aircraft Co, Palmdale, California, USA with RAF role conversion by Marshall of Cambridge (Engineering) Ltd, Cambridge, Cambs. Production and conversions to tanker complete.

Roles & Variants: High capacity long range transport and tanker/transport. Two-point tanker/passenger aircraft (K.1); Two-point tanker/freighter (plus 35 passengers) (KC.1, illustrated below); long range troop transport (C.2 and C.2A). (All conversions based upon civilian model Lockheed TriStar Series 500s.)

First entered service: 1985 (C.2), 1986 (K.1), 1988 (KC.1).

Note: No.216 Squadron maintains detachment of Sigonella, Italy, in support of Operation 'Deliberate Guard' over the former Yugoslavia.

Colour scheme: All white fuselage with dark blue cheatline.

---

216 Sqn Tristar K.1*, KC.1, C.2+, C.2A# **RAF Brize Norton**

Eagle holding a bomb on the fin.

ZD948	ZD949*	ZD950	ZD951*	ZD952	ZD953	ZE704+
ZE705+	ZE706#					

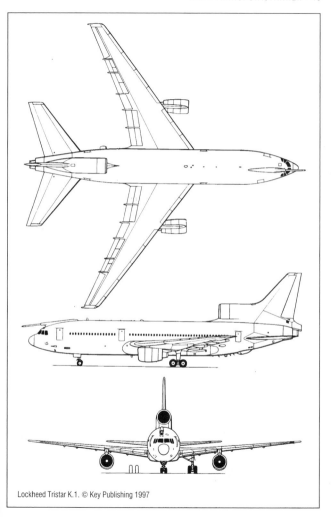

Lockheed Tristar K.1. © Key Publishing 1997

VC-10 C.1, K.2, K.3 and K.4

Specification (C.1K):
Powerplant: Four Rolls-Royce RCo.43 Conway turbojets each of 21,800 st (96.97kN).
Performance: Max speed 581mph (935km/h) at 31,000ft (9,450m). Range with max (passenger/freight) payload 3,898 miles (6,273km).
Weights: Empty 146,000lb (66,224kg). Max take-off (passenger/freighter) 323,000lb (146,510kg).
Dimensions: Span 146ft 2in (44,55m). Length 158ft 8in (48.38m) excluding probe. Height 39ft 6in (12.04m).
Accommodation: 150 passengers, 76 stretcher cases plus attendants or 24,000lb (10,886kg) payload (C.1K), 18 passenger seats (K.2), 17 passenger seats (K.3); approx 120 passengers (K.4).

Manufacturer: British Aircraft Corporation (now British Aerospace) Weybridge, Surrey. Conversions of the K.2, K.3 and K.4 undertaken by BAe at Filton, Glos and C.1K by Flight Refuelling at Bournemouth, Dorset. Production and conversions completed.

Roles & Variants: Long range passenger/freight transport/short range tanker (C.1K) and dedicated long range tanker (K.2, K.3) and passenger transport/short range tanker (K.4). Manufacturer's designation for C.1 Series 1106. The K.2s, K.3s and K.4s converted from civilian standard VC-10 airliners: VC-10 Series 1101, Super VC-10 Series 1154 and Super VC-10 Series 1151 respectively.

First entered service: 1966 (pure transport C.1), 1984 (K.2), 1985 (K.3), 1994 (K.4).

Colour scheme: Entire VC-10 fleet is adopting overall grey with pale blue cheatline. K.2, K.3 and K.4 originally hemp upper surfaces with light grey undersides. C.1 originally white upper fuselage and tail, dark blue cheatline with light aircraft grey lower fuselage and wings.

10 Squadron   VC-10 C.1K   RAF Brize Norton

Winged arrow on fin. Aircraft named after RAF Victoria Cross holders, in serial order: *George Thompson* vc, *Donald Garland* vc/*Thomas Gray* vc, *Kenneth Campbell* vc, *David Lord* vc, *Lance Hawker* vc, *Guy Gibson* vc, *Edward Mannock* vc, *James McCudden* vc, *Albert Ball* vc, *Thomas Mottershead* vc, *James Nicolson* vc, *William Rhodes-Moorhouse* vc, *Arthur Scarf* vc.

XR806	XR807	XR808	XR810	XV101	XV102	XV103
XV104	XV105	XV106	XV107	XV108	XV109	

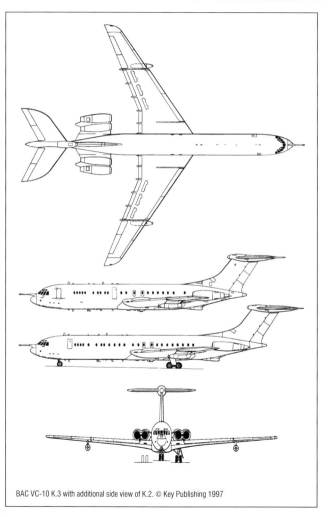

BAC VC-10 K.3 with additional side view of K.2. © Key Publishing 1997

101 Squadron   **VC-10 K.2, K.3*, K.4+**   **RAF Brize Norton**

Lion in (castle) turret with Roman numerals 'CI' in circle on fin. Single-letter codes on fin on hemp-schemed aircraft but possible not to be carried on new grey scheme. See also 1312 Flight below.

A:ZA140   B:ZA141   C:ZA142   D:ZA143   E:ZA144   F:ZA147*   G:ZA148*
H:ZA149*   J:ZA150*   K:ZD230+   L:ZD235+   M:ZD240 +   N:ZD241+
P:ZD242+

1312 Flight   **VC-10 K.4**   **Mount Pleasant Int Airport,**
                                                 Falkland Islands

The Flight operates a VC-10 K.4 on detachment from 101 Squadron, see above, for air-to-air refuelling and a Hercules C.1 (see page 44).

Top left: K.2 ZA140; bottom left K.3 ZA149; above K.4 ZD242 on detachment to 1312 Flight.

No.10 Squadron C.1K XV109 'suckling' a 43 Squadron and a 111 Squadron (foreground) Tornado F.3.

CHINOOK HC.2 and HC.3

Specification (HC.2):

Powerplant: Two Textron Lycoming T55-L-712 turboshafts each of 3,750shp (2,796kW).

Performance: Max speed 185mph (298km/h). Typical operational radius 115 miles (185km).

Weights: Empty 22,379lb (10,151kg). Max take-off 50,000lb (22,679kg).

Dimensions: Both rotors, diameter 60ft 0in (18.29m). Length (fuselage) 51ft 0in (15.54m). Height 18ft 11in (5.77m).

Accommodation/payload: 45 fully equipped troops. 24 stretchers plus attendants. Maximum payload 22,798lb (10,341kg) internally, 13,907lb (6,308kg) externally. Four crew.

Manufacturer: Boeing Helicopters, Philadelphia, Pennsylvania, USA. Production for RAF continuing.

Roles & Variants: Twin rotor heavy transport (HC.2) and special forces support (HC.3) helicopter. The HC.2 and HC.3 are designated Model 414 by Boeing and CH-47D by USAF.

First entered service: 1980 (HC.1).

Notes: Initial deliveries were HC.1s (USAF equivalent CH-47C) later updated to HC.1B with glass fibre rotor blades. New-build HC.2s (CH-47D) plus all surviving HC.1s reworked to HC.2 standard by Boeing. Final HC.2s expected by 1999 (serial numbers ZH891 to ZH896). Eight special forces configured HC.3s (ZH897 to ZH904) for delivery in 1998 and possibly destined for 27 Squadron. The Chinook force maintains a detachment in Split, Bosnia, in support of the peace-keeping force there.

Odiham, Hants, has become the RAF's Chinook centre with 18 Squadron completing its relocation from Laarbruch, Germany by July 1997. Five Chinooks will move from 7 Squadron to No.18. Both 7 and 18 Squadrons have operated Westland Gazelle HT.3s as 'hacks', coming from 2 Flying Training School at Shawbury, Shropshire. With the wind down of this unit, it is not known if this practise will continue.

Colour scheme: Overall drab green.

See also: 'Test & Trials' (page 143).

---

7 Squadron　　　　**Chinook HC.2**　　　　**RAF Odiham**

Star constellation of Ursa Minor on the rear rotor pylon. Two-letter codes beginning 'E' in black on the rear rotor pylon. See 'Notes' above.

EA:ZD980	EB:ZA675	ED:ZA681	EE:ZD984	EF:ZA674	EG:ZA677	EH:ZD574
EI:ZD983	EJ:ZA704	EK:ZD982	EL:ZA684	EM:ZA713	EN:ZA714	EP:ZA720
EQ:ZA709	ER:ZA712	ET:ZA711	EV:ZA707	ZA673		

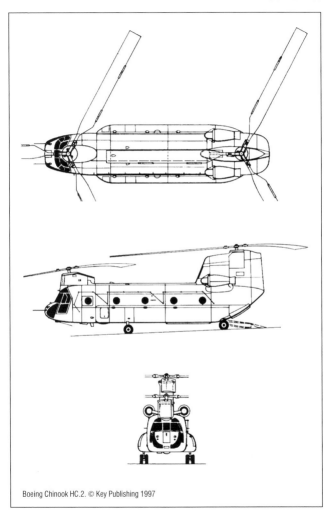

Boeing Chinook HC.2. © Key Publishing 1997

18 Squadron   Chinook HC.2   RAF Odiham
Red Pegasus, the winged horse, on black circle on the rear rotor pylon. Two-letter codes
beginning 'B' in black on the rear rotor pylon. See 'Notes' above.
BB:ZA671   BC:ZA708   BE:ZA705   BF:ZA670   BG:ZA682

27 (R) Squadron   Chinook HC.2   RAF Odiham
Elephant in circle with bar in black on the rotor pylon. Two-letter codes beginning 'N' in black
on the rear rotor pylon. The unit currently acts as the Chinook and Puma (see page 60) conversion unit. See 'Notes' above.
NS:ZH775   NU:ZH776   NX:ZA673   NY:ZH777   NZ:ZD575

78 Squadron   **Chinook HC.2**   **Mount Pleasant Int Airport, Falkland Islands**

Heraldic tiger on black disc on rear rotor pylon. Single-letter code in black on the rear rotor pylon. The unit also operates Sea King HAR.3s (see page 66).
C:ZA679   D:ZA683

Detail views of a No.27 (R) Chinook. Below, left: Radar warning receiver alongside code letters; aft of jet exhaust, flare dispenser; below exhaust, infra-red jammer. Below, right: Door-mounted, Gatling-type machine-gun.

GRIFFIN HT.1

Specification:
Powerplant: One Pratt & Whitney Canada PT6T-3B-1 Turbo TwinPac coupled turboshaft of 1,400shp (1,044kW).
Performance: Max speed 161mph (258km/h). Range 432 miles (695km).
Weights: Empty 6,470lb (2,935kg). Max take-off 11,900lb (5,397kg).
Dimensions: Rotor diameter 46ft 0in (14.02m). Length 42ft 4¾in (12.92) fuselage. Height 14ft 2¼in (4.32m).

Manufacturer: Bell Helicopter Textron, Fort Worth, Texas, USA. Production continuing.

Roles & Variants: Advanced training helicopter. Manufacturer's designation Model 412EP.

First entered service: 1997, civilian contractor owned and operated.

Notes: Operated within the Defence Helicopter Flying School (run by FBS Ltd, a combined operation by FR Aviation, Bristow Helicopters and SERCO) to train helicopter pilots for all three services. DHFS officially came into operation at Shawbury, Shropshire, on 1st April 1997.

Colour scheme: Gloss black fuselage with gloss yellow upper fuselage.

See also: The essentially similar Bell 212s operated by 7 Flight Army Air Corps in Brunei (page 132).

60 (R) Squadron	Griffin HT.1	DHFS Shawbury RAF Valley

 Disbanded at Benson 26th March 1997 (operating Westland Wessex HC.2s) to become the 'shadow' squadron for the RAF element of the DHFS (see 'Notes' above) with the 'umbrella' title of 2 Flying Training School. Single-letter codes in white on fuselage sides, that will spell out SIXTY RULE when deliveries complete! (Three codes won as *Air Forces UK* closed for press.) DHFS will also have within it the CFS Helicopter Squadron. In particular 60 Squadron is responsible for the Griffins which are used for the RAF's advanced training requirements. DHFS also undertake the work of the SAR Training Unit, which disbanded at RAF Valley in April 1997, having operated Wessex HC.2s. Aircraft 'U', 'L' and 'E" will be hoist-equipped and probably permanently based at Valley.

S:ZJ234   I:ZJ235   X:ZJ236   ZJ237   ZJ238   ZJ239   ZJ240
ZJ241   ZJ242

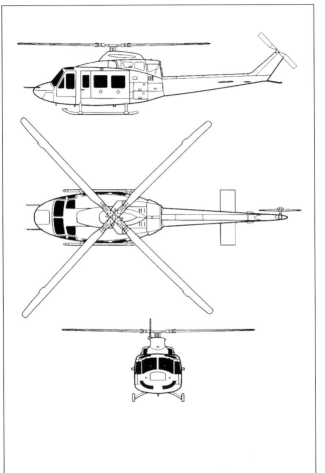

Bell Griffin HT.1. Note that the Bell 212 is essentially similar, see page 132.
Pete West © Midland Publishing 1997

PUMA HC.1

Specification:

Powerplant: Two Turboméca Turmo III C4 turboshafts each of 1,435shp (1,070kW).

Performance: Max speed 169mph (272km/h) at sea
level. Typical range 310 miles (500km).

Weights: Empty 7,403lb (3,358kg). Max take-off
14,110lb (6,400kg).

Dimensions: Rotor diameter 49ft 2½in (15.00m).
Length 46ft 1½in (14.06m) fuselage. Height 16ft
10½in (5.14m).

Accommodation/Payload: 16 fully equipped troops,
or six stretchers plus attendants. Max 5,511lb
(2,500kg) underslung load.

Manufacturer: Sud Aviation/Aérospatiale (now
Eurocopter), Marignane, France with co-production
and assembly by Westland Helicopters, Yeovil,
Somerset, UK. Production of the SA.330 Puma
completed, production of the much-developed
AS.532 Cougar continuing.

Roles & Variants: Medium capacity transport helicopter. Manufacturer's designation SA.330E.

Notes: No.27 (R) Squadron at Odiham is thought to
be giving up its Pumas and they and the training task
will move to Benson, Oxfordshire, in 1998.

Colour scheme: Two-tone grey camouflage overall.

See also: 'Test & Trials' (page 143).

---

27 (R) Squadron   Puma HC.1   RAF Odiham

Two-letter codes beginning 'N' in black on the tail boom. The unit currently acts as the Puma
and Chinook (see page 54) conversion unit. See 'Notes' above.

NC:XW200   NE:XW202   NJ:XW227   NK:XW226   XW211

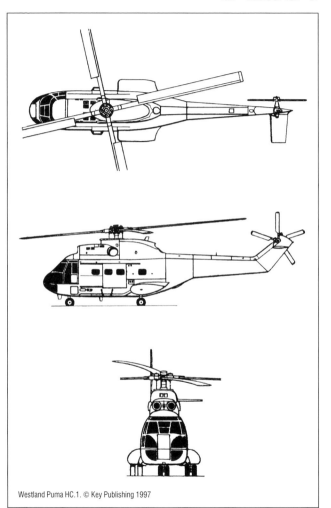

Westland Puma HC.1. © Key Publishing 1997

33 Squadron   Puma HC.1   RAF Benson

Squadron emblem a hart's head, not seen on the unit's Pumas for some time. Codes worn relate to previous units.

| XW201 | NG:XW206 | XW207 | XW208 | NH:XW209 | XW212 |
| XW213 | XW221 | XW223 | XW229 | XW232 | XW237 |

72 Squadron   Puma HC.1   RAF Aldergrove

Swift on blue circle flanked by blue and red bars below cockpit. Two -letter codes beginning 'A' are starting to be applied, other codes worn relate to previous units. Deliveries of Pumas started early in 1997, Also operate the Westland Wessex HC.2 (see page 70).

AA:XW204 AB:XW214 AD:XW224 AE:XW235 XW220

230 Squadron **Puma HC.1** **RAF Aldergrove**

Tiger's head on black pentagon below cockpit. Codes worn relate to previous units.

XW198	NB:XW199	NK:XW217	XW219	XW222	NM:XW231
XW234	NO:XW236	BZ:ZA934	NR:ZA935	ZA936	ZA937
ZA938	DN:ZA939	ZA940			

SEA KING HAR.3, HAR.3A

Specification:

Powerplant: Two Rolls-Royce Gnome H.1400-1T turboshafts each of 1,660shp (1,238kW).

Performance: Max speed 140mph (226km/h). Ferry range 1,082 miles (1,742km). Typical operational radius 280 miles (450km).

Weights: Empty 11,891lb (5,393kg). Max take-off 21,500lb (9,752kg).

Dimensions: Rotor diameter 62ft 0in (18.90m). Length 55ft 10in (17.02m) fuselage. Height 16ft 10in (5.13m).

Accommodation: Up to 18 passengers, or six stretchers plus attendant. Four crew.

Manufacturer: Westland Helicopters Ltd, Yeovil, Somerset. Production nearly complete.

Role & Variants: Long range, high capacity search and rescue helicopter (HAR.3) and with enhanced all-weather search capability (HAR.3A). Highly developed, licensed produced derivative of the Sikorsky SH-3D Sea King (Model S-61).

First entered service: 1977.

Notes: Problems in software of the HAR.3A updated flight computer have delayed the phase in of the type and the eventual replacement of the Wessex HC.2 from search and rescue (SAR) service.

Colour scheme: UK based aircraft overall SAR yellow. Falklands-based examples medium grey overall (known as 'Combat SAR').

See also: Fleet Air Arm operates the Sea King extensively (see page 114) and also 'Test & Trials' (page 143).

22 Squadron	Sea King HAR.3, HAR.3A*	RAF St Mawgan
'A' Flight		RM Chivenor
'B' Flight		AAC Wattisham
'C' Flight		RAF Valley

Greek letter 'π' over a Maltese cross on the forward fuselage. HQ at St Mawgan with Sea King Flights as above. 'A' Flight became the first operational unit with the HAR.3A in June 1997 with the 'C' Flight at Valley following.

XZ588   ZE369   ZH540*   ZH542*   ZH544*

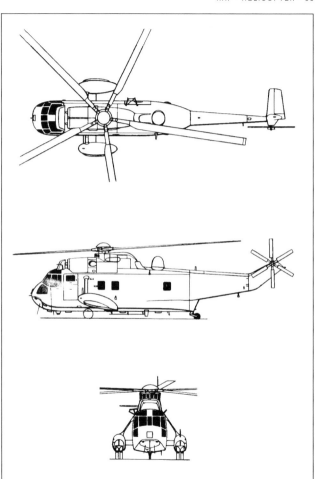

Westland Sea King HAR.3. Naval variants are essentially of the same fomat, see page 114.
© Key Publishing 1997

78 Squadron   **Sea King HAR.3**   **Mount Pleasant Int Airport, Falkland Islands**

Heraldic tiger on black disc on forward fuselage. Single-letter code in black on fuselage – note *both* Sea Kings carry the same code!. The unit also operates Chinook HC.2s (see page 54).
XZ586   XZ599

202 Squadron   **Sea King HAR.3**   **RAF Boulmer**
    'A' Flight   **RAF Boulmer**
    'D' Flight   **RAF Lossiemouth**
    'E' Flight   **Army Leconfield**

Mallard in flight on white disc on forward fuselage. HQ at Boulmer.

XZ585	XZ589	XZ592	XZ596	XZ597	XZ598
ZE368	ZE370				

203 (R) Squadron   **Sea King HAR.3,**
                                       HAR.3A*   **RAF St Mawgan**

Seahorse on white disc on forward fuselage. The RAF Sea King Training Unit was renumbered as 203 (R) Squadron on 1st November 1996.

XZ590	XZ591	XZ593	XZ595	ZH543*	ZH545*

TWIN SQUIRREL

Specification:

Powerplant: Two Allison 250-C20F turboshafts each of 420shp (313kW).

Performance: Max speed 137mph (221km/h) at sea level. Range 432 miles (695km) without reserves.

Weights: Empty 2,900lb (1,315kg). Max take-off 5,600lb (2,540kg).

Dimensions: Rotor diameter 35ft 0¾in (10.69m). Length 35ft 10½in (10.93m). Height 10ft 3½in (3.14m).

Manufacturer: Aérospatiale (now Eurocopter), Marignane, France.

Role & Variants: Twin-engined five to six seat VIP helicopter. Manufacturer's designation AS.355F₁, known in France as the Ecureuil and in the USA as the Twinstar. Note, the designation HCC.1 has been quoted for these helicopters but is not confirmed.

First entered service: 1996.

Notes: Contractor owned and operated within the 32 Squadron fleet.

Colour scheme: Overall white with dark blue cheatline, red tail fin and tail rotor transmission spine.

See also: Defence Helicopter Flying School uses the essentially similar single-engined AS.350BB (see page 140).

32 (The Royal) Squadron   Twin Squirrel   RAF Northolt

Unit badge, a hunting horn, on the doors. The unit also operates BAe HS.125s (page 39), BAe 146s (page 40) and Wessex HCC.4s (page 70).

ZJ139   ZJ140

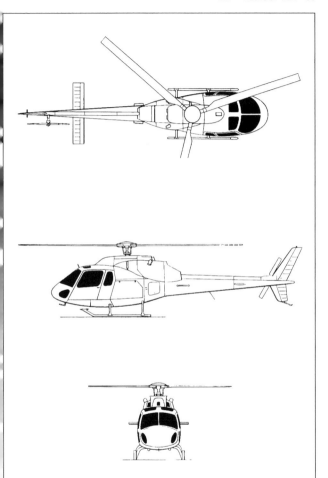

Aérospatiale Twin Squirrel. See also pages 120 and 140 for the broadly similar Squirrel HT.1.
© Key Publishing 1997

WESSEX HC.2, HCC.4

Specification (HC.2):

Powerplant: Two Rolls-Royce Gnome Mk.110/111 turboshafts each of 1,350shp (1,007kW).

Performance: Max speed 132mph (212km/h) at sea level. Ferry range 645 miles (1,040km).

Weights: Empty 8,304lb (3,767kg). Max take-off 13,500lb (6,123kg).

Dimensions: Rotor diameter 56ft 0in (17.07m). Length 48ft 4½in (14.74m) fuselage.

Accommodation/Payload: 16 fully equipped troops, up to 20 passengers in SAR role. Underslung load 4,000lb (1,814kg).

Manufacturer: Westland Helicopters Ltd, Yeovil, Somerset. Production completed.

Role & Variants: Medium transport and search and rescue (SAR) helicopter (HC.2) and VIP transport (HCC.4). Highly developed, licensed produced derivative of the Sikorsky H-34 Choctaw (manufacturer's designation S-58).

First entered service: 1964 (HC.2), 1969 (HCC.4).

Notes: The long-serving Wessex was replaced in the SAR role by the Sea King HAR.3 and HAR.3A during 1997 (page 62) but looks set to continue with 72 Squadron in Northern Ireland until 2001 when the Merlin HC.3 arrives (see 'The Future' on page 148). There is a pressing need to replace the two HCC.4s with 32 (The Royal) Squadron and again the Merlin has been quoted as a possible replacement. Much more likely is a version of the AS.532 Cougar (a development of the SA.330 Puma, see page 60), probably contractor owned and operated.

Colour scheme: No.32 Squadron overall gloss red with dark blue cheatline. No.72 Squadron two tone green overall. No.84 Squadron overall medium grey.

See also: 'Test & Trials' page 143.

---

32 (The Royal) Squadron   Wessex HCC.4   RAF Northolt

The unit also operates BAe HS.125s (page 39), BAe 146s (page 40) and Twin Squirrels (page 68). See 'Notes' above.

XV732   XV733

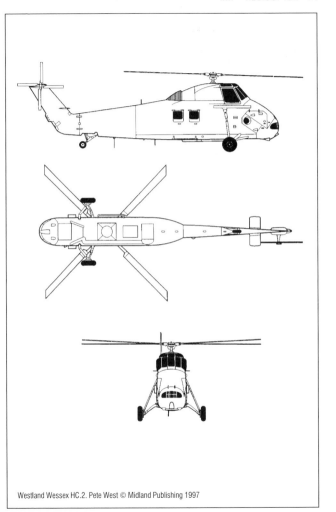

Westland Wessex HC.2. Pete West © Midland Publishing 1997

72 Squadron   Wessex HC.2   RAF Aldergrove

Single-letter codes in black on the fuselage. The unit also operates Puma HC.1s (see page 60).

| C:XV725 | E:XR529 | F:XR497 | G:XR525 | H:XV721 | I:XT676 | J:XV726 |
| L:XR511 | Q:XV723 | S:XT668 | V:XR506 | X:XR498 |

84 Squadron   Wessex HC.2   RAF Akrotiri, Cyprus

Black scorpion on nose. Black 'codes' on tail rotor fin from the suits of a pack of playing cards, including the joker*. Note, illustration below shows previously-operated Wessex HU.5C.

♥:XR588   ♦:XT680   ♣:XV730   ♠:XS675   *:XR504

During June 1997, the long familiar all-yellow Wessex HC.2 bowed out of RAF service. Last operated at Valley, the type served with the SAR Training Unit until its disbandment in April 1997 (its role being taken on by the DHFS, see page 58). No.22 Squadron 'C' Flight used the faithful type until receiving the first Sea King HAR.3s in June 1997.

Also in June 1997, No.28 Squadron disbanded at Kai Tak in Hong Kong, as part of the British withdrawal from the former colony. There six Wessex HC.2s were then dismantled and crated for shipment to Uruguay, who acquired them for their air force.

Recently withdrawn from use by DTEO at Boscombe Down is HU.5 XS509. This leaves only HC.2 XR503 with the DRA as the only serving 'Test & Trials' Wessex.

BULLDOG T.1

....

Specification:
Powerplant: One Textron Lycoming IO-360-A1B6 piston engine of 200hp (149kW).
Performance: Max speed 150mph (241km/h) at sea level. Range 622 miles (1,001km).
Weights: Empty 1,430lb (649kg). Max take-off 2,350lb (1,066kg).
Dimensions: Span 33ft 0in (10.06m). Length 23ft 3in (7.09m). Height 7ft 5¾in (2.28m).

Manufacturer: Scottish Aviation (now British Aerospace), Prestwick, Scotland. Production completed.

Roles & Variants: Two-seat primary trainer and air experience aircraft.

First entered service: 1973.

Notes: Replacement of the Bulldog for the newly-combined University Air Squadron and Air Experience Flight operation is expected to come to a conclusion in October 1997 and, if successful, should see the rapid withdrawal of the type and its replacement by a fleet of contractor owned and operated, civilian-registered types. (It would then seem unlikely that the pooled Bulldog Squadron within No.3 Flying Training School would survive, probably borrowing further from the JEFTS fleet – see page 82.) The competition appears to be down to the Slingsby Firefly (page 82) and the Grob G.115 Heron (page 122). Basing, fleet size, etc could well change under the new regime.

Colour scheme: Overall gloss black with yellow fuselage tops was being introduced but was halted in mid-1997 – more writing on the wall for the Bulldog?. Bulk of the fleet still in white upper fuselage, red lower fuselage and wingtips scheme.

3 Flying Training School   Bulldog T.1   RAF Cranwell
One and two-digit codes carried on the nose and fin. No.3 FTS, which reports to the RAF College Commandant, controls numbers 45 (R) and 55 (R) Squadrons (see pages 88 and 78) as well as the Central Flying School (CFS) Bulldog Squadron. Additionally, the RAF College Air Squadron uses aircraft from the Bulldog Squadron, in addition to Fireflies from the JEFTS at nearby Barkston Heath – see page 82 – as required. (See 'Notes' above.)

1:XX634	2:XX617	3:XX654	4:XX686	5:XX630	6:XX661	7:XX561
8:XX688	9:XX698	10:XX513	(12):XX638	13:XX687	14:XX519	15:XX540
16:XX667	17:XX700	18:XX538	19:XX562			

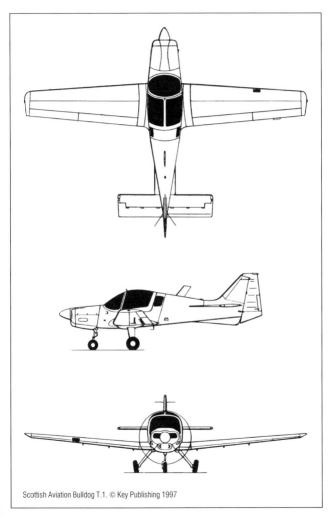

Scottish Aviation Bulldog T.1. © Key Publishing 1997

University Air Squadrons/Air Experience Flights

Aircraft use a variety of coding systems and squadron markings. The two Leuchars-based units are currently operating the same numerical coding system but have been split into the two different UAS for the listing below. The Royal Military College at Shrivenham has an Air Squadron and they are assigned to the Oxford UAS for flying training.

The names used below are not always the current titles for the units, the following is a list of those units where there are differences:

Aberdeen, Dundee & St Andrews Universities Air Sqn
East Midlands Universities Air Sqn
Universities of Glasgow & Strathclyde Air Sqn
Manchester & Salford Universities Air Sqn

University of Wales Air Sqn
University of Birmingham Air Sqn
University of London Air Sqn
Yorkshire Universities Air Sqn

Aberdeen, Dundee & St Andrews UAS **Bulldog T.1** **RAF Leuchars**
05:XX527   06:XX522   07:XX693   XX666

Birmingham UAS (8 AEF) **Bulldog T.1** **RAF Cosford**
A:XX558   B:XX534   C:XX670   D:XX671   E:XX672   F:XX699   G:XX521

Bristol UAS (3 AEF) **Bulldog T.1** **RAF Colerne**
A:XX692   B:XX655   C:XX656   D:XX689   E:XX653   F:XX541   G:XX713
H:XX697   J:XX628   K:XX640   XX689 illustrated above, right.

Cambridge UAS (5 AEF) **Bulldog T.1** **Cambridge Airport**
A:XX658   B:XX518   C:XX516   D:XX624   E:XX532   F:XX529   S:XX659
U:XX657

East Lowlands UAS **Bulldog T.1** **RAF Leuchars**
01:XX663   02:XX537   03:XX525   04:XX664

East Midlands UAS (7 AEF) **Bulldog T.1** **RAF Newton**
A:XX520   E:XX694   M:XX556   S:XX535   U:XX704   π:XX702
XX520 illustrated below, right

Glasgow & Strathclyde UAS **Bulldog T.1** **Glasgow Airport**
XX559   XX560   XX611   XX665

Liverpool UAS **Bulldog T.1** **RAF Woodvale**
A:XX690   L:XX539   S:XX696   U:XX555   X:XX523

London UAS (6 AEF) **Bulldog T.1** **RAF Benson**
01:XX544   02:XX639   03:XX546   04:XX524   05:XX547   06:XX548   07:XX553
08:XX552   09:XX554   10:XX691

Manchester UAS (10 AEF)   **Bulldog T.1**   **RAF Woodvale**
1:XX668   2:XX615   3:XX616   4:XX515   5:XX710   6:XX536

Northumbrian UAS (11 AEF) **Bulldog T.1**   **RAF Leeming**
T:XX619   U:XX533   V:XX629   W:XX631   X:XX633   Y:XX636   Z:XX550

Oxford UAS   **Bulldog T.1**   **RAF Benson**
A:XX695   B:XX614   C:XX526   D:XX528   E:XX551   S:XX711

Southampton UAS (2 AEF)   **Bulldog T.1**   **DTEO Boscombe Down**
01:XX706   02:XX701   03:XX708   04:XX707   05:XX705   06:XX549   07:XX627

Wales UAS   **Bulldog T.1**   **RAF St Athan**
01:XX625   02:XX626   03:XX612   04:XX531

Yorkshire UAS (9 AEF)   **Bulldog T.1**   **RAF Church Fenton**
A:XX632   B:XX622   C:XX620   D:XX714   E:XX709   F:XX543   G:XX621

DOMINIE T.1

Specification:
Powerplant: Two Rolls-Royce Viper Mk.301 turbojets each of 3,120lb st (13.88kN).
Performance: Max speed 472mph (760km/h). Range 1,338 miles (2,153km).
Weights: Empty 10,100lb (4,581kg). Max take-off 21,200lb (9,616kg).
Dimensions: Span 47ft 0in (14.33m). Length 47ft 5in (14.45m). Height 16ft 6in (5.03m).

Manufacturer: Hawker Siddeley (now British Aerospace), Hawarden, North Wales. Production of series completed, design rights now owned by Raytheon and produced in the USA.

Role & Variants: Twin-jet navigation 'flying classroom' accommodating three students, instructor and two flight crew. Manufacturer's designation HS.125 Series 2. Note that recent extensive reworking by Marshall of Cambridge originally was thought to have brought about the designation T.2, but this is no longer the case.

First entered service: 1965.

Notes: Eleven aircraft updated from 1993, remainder of the fleet relegated to ground instructional duties.

Colour scheme: Gloss back overall with white top decking to fuselage being introduced. Others White upper fuselage with red cheatline, wingtips and tail areas with grey under fuselage.

See also: Essentially similar HS.125 used by 32 Squadron, see page 39. See also 'Test & Trials', page 143.

55 (R) Squadron   Dominie T.1   RAF Cranwell
Single-letter code carried on the fin only on black aircraft and on nose and fin on red aircraft. Part of 3 Flying Training School, see page 74 for structure details. The Dominie Squadron of 3 FTS was renumbered as No.55 (R) on 1st November 1996.

A:XS712   C:XS713   D:XS727   E:XS728   F:XS739   H:XS730   J:XS731
K:XS737   L:XS711   M:XS709   S:XS736

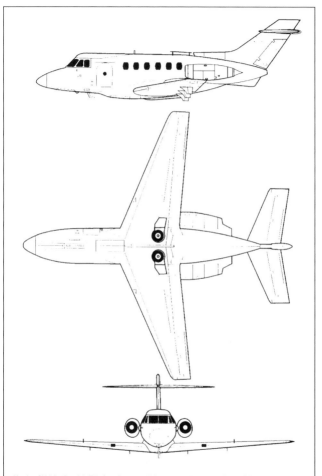

Hawker Siddeley Dominie T.1. See also page 39 for the broadly similar HS.125 CC.2 and CC.3.
Pete West © Midland Publishing 1997

FALCON 20C, 'DC AND 'E

Specification (20DC):
Powerplant: Two General Electric CF700-2B turbofans each of 4,250lb st (18.90kN).
Performance: Max speed 541mph (870km/h) at 30,000ft 9,144m). Range approx 1,000 miles (1,603km).
Weights: Empty 13,000lb (5,896kg). Max take-off approx 27,500lb (12,474kg).
Dimensions: Span 50ft 6in (15.39m). Length 56ft 3in (17.14m). Height 17ft 4in (5.28m).
Accommodation: Flightcrew of three, up to ten passengers in non-specialist configuration. Four wing hardpoints for a variety of pods.

Manufacturer: Dassault Aviation, Mérignac, France. Production completed.

Roles & Variants: Twin-jet weapons and systems facilities trainer. Internal fits and pylon-mounted pods permitting electronic warfare threat and countermeasures simulation; target facilities and gun-laying work; radar calibration etc. FR Aviation uses three versions of the Falcon 20 executive jet, the 20C former Canadian Armed Forces, 20DC former Federal Express small package freighter and the 20E civilian executive. Also known in France as the Mystère 20 and in the USA as the Fan Jet Falcon 20.

First entered service: 1986 (ECM contract with RAF from 1994)

Notes: Contractor owned and operated, by FR Aviation, based at Bournemouth and Tees-side Airports and elsewhere as needed. Under contract to both the RAF and the Royal Navy for a variety of simulated threat/countermeasure and target facilities training.

Colour scheme: Overall white with two-tone blue trim.

See also: Operated also for the Royal Navy along with Cessna 441s, see page 120.

FR Aviation		Falcon 20C*, 'DC, 'E+			Bournemouth/Tees-side	
All civilian registered.						
G-FFRA	G-FRAD+	G-FRAE+	G-FRAF+	G-FRAH	G-FRAI+	G-FRAJ
G-FRAK	G-FRAL	G-FRAM	G-FRAO	G-FRAP	G-FRAR	G-FRAS*
G-FRAT*	G-FRAU*	G-FRAW*				

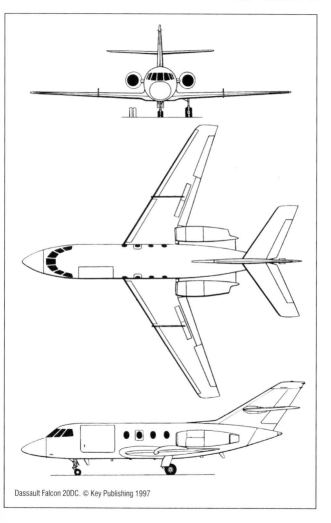

Dassault Falcon 20DC. © Key Publishing 1997

FIREFLY

Specification (T.67M Mk.II):
Powerplant: One Textron Lycoming AEIO-320-D1B piston engine of 160hp (119kW).
Performance: Max speed 157mph (252km/h) at sea level. Range 608 miles (980km) with reserves.
Weights: Empty 1,450lb (658kg). Max take-off 2,100lb (952kg).
Dimensions: Span 34ft 9in (10.59m). Length 24ft 0¼in (7.32m). Height 7ft 9in (2.36m).

Manufacturer: Slingsby Aviation, Kirbymoorside, North Yorkshire. Deliveries to Hunting Aviation to be completed mid-1997. Production continuing.

Role & Variants: Two-seat primary trainer. Manufacturer's designation T.67. T.67M Mk II with 160hp (119kW), T.67M-200 with 200hp (149kW) AEIO-360-A1E and T.67M-260 with 260hp (195kW) AETO-540-D4A5 engine.

First entered service: 1995.

Notes: Contractor owned and operated by Hunting Aviation. From 1st April 1997 a tri-service school, training Army Air Corps, Fleet Air Arm and RAF intake pilots. See under Bulldog, page 74.

Colour scheme: Overall white with dark blue cheatline and fin/rudder with red wingtips. Adopting overall yellow fuselage and inner wings with black tail, wingtips and cowling.

JEFTS   Firefly Mk.II, -200+, -260*

RAF Barkston Heath and RAF Newton

All civilian registered. JEFTS comes under HQ EFTS which, like 3 FTS, reports to the RAF College Commandant (see page 74 for structure details). Newton is a satellite field.

G–BLVI	G–BNSO	G–BNSP	G–BNSR	G–BONT	G–BUUA	G–BUUB
G–BUUC	G–BUUD	G–BUUE	G–BUUF	G–BUUG	G–BUUI	G–BUUJ
G–BUUK	G–BUUL	G–BWXA*	G–BWXB*	G–BWXC*	G–BWXD*	G–BWXE*
G–BWXF*	G–BWXG*	G–BWXH*	G–BWXI*	G–BWXJ*	G–BWXK*	G–BWXL*
G–BWXM*	G–BWXN*	G–BWXO*	G–BWXP*	G–BWXR*	G–BWXS*	G–BWXT*
G–BWXU*	G–BWXV*	G–BWXW*	G–BWXX*	G–BWXY*	G–BWXZ*	
G–HONG+	G–KONG+					

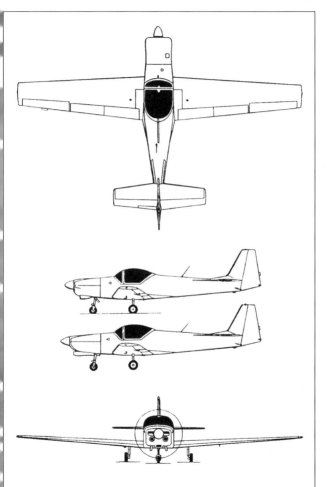

Slingsby T.67M Firefly Mk.II and, lower side view, T.67M-260 Firefly. © Key Publishing 1997

HAWK T.1, T.1A

Specification (T.1):
Powerplant: One Rolls-Royce/Turboméca Adour Mk.151-01 of 5,200lb st (23.13kN).
Performance: Max speed 645mph (1,038km/h) at 11,000ft (3,355m). Ferry range 1,509 miles (2,428km).
Weights: Empty 8,040lb (3,647kg). Max take-off 12,566lb (5,700kg).
Dimensions: Span 30ft 9¾in (9.39m). Length 36ft 7¾in (11.17m). Height 13ft 1¼in (3.99m).
Armament: (T.1A) One 30mm ADEN cannon in centreline gun pod. Two AIM-9L Sidewinder air-to-air missiles on wing stations.

Manufacturer: Hawker Siddeley (now British Aerospace), Dunsfold, Surrey. Production of the T.1/T.1A completed, production of the more advanced Hawk 100 and single-seater Hawk 200 continuing at BAe Warton, Lancs.

Roles & Variants: Two-seat advanced jet trainer

(T.1). Two-seat advanced weapons trainer with limited point-defence war role capability (T.1A). Manufacturer's designation HS.1182.

First entered service: 1976 (T.1), 1985 (T.1A).

Notes: No.100 Squadron is a tri-service target facilities unit employed widely in support of air exercises etc. Its place within the 'central' RAF is currently under review and may become a 'contractorised' operation. Since the introduction of dedicated roles for each Reserve (R) squadron and the grounding order issued on all Hawks in early 1997, previous squadron allocations and codes have become very fluid, with aircraft retaining unit badges, but not codes.

Colour scheme: Overall light grey scheme giving way to overall gloss black with white on the upper wing surfaces. Red Arrows aircraft overall red with white and blue trim.

See also: Fleet Air Arm operates the Hawk in the fleet requirements role, see page 121. See also 'Test & Trials', page 143.

19 (R) Squadron   Hawk T.1, T.1A*   RAF Valley

Dolphin on circle on fin. Two-letter codes beginning 'P' on fin. This is the Central Flying School (CFS) Hawk Squadron and is part of 4 Flying Training School, see below. Aircraft presented in serial number order, see 'Notes' above.

XX169	XX174	PQ:XX178	XX179	XX187*	XX225	PK:XX236
XX238	XX240	PD:XX278*	PE:XX281*	XX287*	XX299	XX321*
XX324*	XX326*	XX330*	XX338			

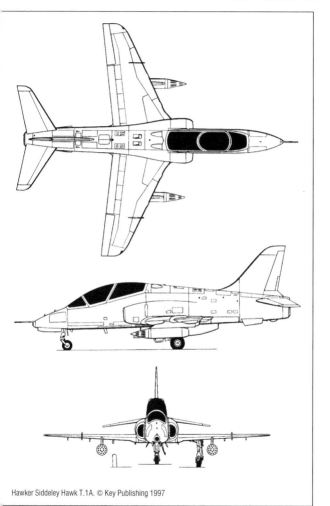

Hawker Siddeley Hawk T.1A. © Key Publishing 1997

74 (R) Squadron   Hawk T.1, T.1A*   RAF Valley

Tiger's head on fin on some aircraft. Yellow and black triangles in bar on engine intake. Two-letter codes beginning 'T' on fin. Aircraft presented in serial number order, see 'Notes' above. Part of 4 Flying Training School, see below.

XX186*	TI:XX188*	XX199*	XX202*	TJ:XX222*	XX226	XX230
XX232	XX235	XX244	XX246*	XX303*	XX318*	XX319*
TD:XX323*	XX329*	XX332*	TV:XX339*	XX345*	DN:XX348*	
TC:XX350*	XX351*					

100 Squadron   Hawk T.1*, T.1A   RAF Leeming

Skull and crossbones on nose or fin. Blue and yellow chequers flanking fuselage roundel, or on fin/rudder. Two-letter codes beginning 'C' on fin. Aircraft presented in serial number order, see 'Notes' above and Joint Forward Air Control Standards & Training Unit below.

CB:XX193	CC:XX228*	CD:XX335	CE:XX325*	CF:XX200	CH:XX285	CI:XX289
CJ:XX248	CK:XX331	CL:XX284	CM:XX247	CN:XX265	CO:XX194	CP:XX352
(CQ):XX282*						

208 (R) Squadron   Hawk T.1, T.1A*   RAF Valley

A winged eye on the fin. Blue/yellow arrowhead on nose. Two-letter codes beginning 'D' on fin.
Aircraft presented in serial number order, see 'Notes' above. Part of 4 Flying Training School,
see below.

XX156	XX158	XX161	XX167	XX171	DS:XX176	XX181
DT:XX191*	DD:XX195	XX204*	XX218*	XX224	XX231	XX239
XX249	XX256*	DY:XX283	XX309	XX312	XX313	
DU:XX314*	DL:XX317*	XX349*				

JFACS & TU   Hawk T.1   RAF Leeming

Joint Forward Air Control Standards & Training Unit. Anchor, rifle and wings within circle on fin,
100 Squadron chequers either side of roundel. A part of 100 Squadron, see above. Tri-service
unit training forward air controllers.
CA:XX168   CG:XX250

Central Flying School   **Hawk T.1, T.1A**   **RAF Cranwell**
Headquartered at Cranwell, the CFS provides instructor training for the RAF. Hawks at Valley with 19 (R) Squadron (see page 84), and one aircraft on permanent detachment to Cranwell for HQ use. Bulldogs are at Cranwell, operated with 3 FTS – see page 74. The Helicopter Squadron is now within the DHFS make-up - see 58.

4 Flying Training School   **Hawk T.1, T.1A**   **RAF Valley**
Hawks operated under the banners of 19 (R), 74 (R) and 208 (R) Squadrons – see above.

St Athan Station Flight   **Hawk T.1**   **RAF St Athan**
Two Hawks employed as 'hacks' for ferry pilots from the maintenance and storage unit.
XX172   XX184

Red Arrows – RAF Aerobatic Team

			Hawk T.1, T.1A*		**RAF Cranwell**	
XX227*	XX233	XX237	XX252*	XX253*	XX260*	XX264*
XX266*	XX292	XX294	XX306*	XX307	XX308	

JETSTREAM T.1

Specification:
Powerplant: Two Turboméca Astazou XVID turbo-props each of 913shp (681kW).
Performance: Max speed 282mph (454km/h) at 10,000ft (3,050,). Range 1,382 miles (2,224km).
Weights: Empty 7,683lb (3,495kg). Max take-off 12,566lb (5,700kg).
Dimensions: Span 52ft 0in (15.85m). Length 47ft 1½in (14.37m). Height 17ft 5½in (5.32m).

Manufacturer: Scottish Aviation (now British Aerospace), Prestwick, Scotland. Production completed.

Role & Variants: Multi-engined pilot trainer with auxiliary transport role. Initial manufacturer's designation HP.137.

First entered service: 1973.

Colour scheme: White upper decking and tail with red cheatline, sections of tail, outer wings, light aircraft grey lower fuselage and wings. Fleet reported to be adopting overall gloss black with white top decking to fuselage, but as of June 1997, no examples so painted.

See also: Royal Navy employs the Jetstream as a trainer and communications aircraft, see page 124. See also 'Test & Trials' page 143.

45 (Reserve) Squadron   Jetstream T.1   RAF Cranwell

Winged camel within circle under the cockpit of 'red' examples. Single-letter code in white on the fin. Part of 3 Flying Training School, see page 74 for structure details.

A/XX492   B/XX494   C/XX495   D/XX496   E/XX497   F/XX498   G/XX499
H/XX500   J/XX482   K/XX491   L/XX493

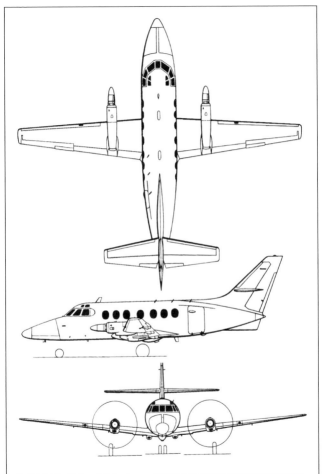

Scottish Aviation Jetstream T.1. See also page 124 for the essentially similar Jetstream T.2 and T.3.
© Key Publishing 1997

TUCANO T.1

Specification:
Powerplant: One Garrett TPE331-12B turboprop of 1,100shp (820kW).
Performance: Max speed 319mph (513km/h) at 10,000ft (3,050m). Range 1,099 miles (1,767km).
Weights: Empty 4,872lb (2,210kg). Max take-off 6,470lb (2,935kg).
Dimensions: Span 37ft 0in (11.28m). Length 32ft 4¼in (9.86m). Height 11ft 1¾in (3.40m).

Manufacturer: Short Brothers plc, Sydenham, Belfast, Northern Ireland. Production complete.

Role & Variants: Two-seat basic trainer. Considerably developed version of the Brazilian EMBRAER EMB-312 Tucano.

First entered service: 1988.

Notes: RAF production amounted to 130 aircraft, large numbers held in reserve store at Shawbury, Shropshire. Aircraft frequently exchanged to keep flying hours even.

Colour scheme: White upper fuselage, red lower fuselage, tailplane and wingtips. Fleet adopting overall gloss black with white upper wings.

See also: 'Test & Trials' page 143.

1 Flying Training School	Tucano T.1	RAF Linton-on-Ouse
CFS Tucano Squadron	Tucano T.1	RAF Topcliffe

Aircraft wear 'last three' of their serial number on the nose and fin. No.1 FTS supplies the Tucano element of the CFS syllabus (see under Bulldog, page 74 for details of CFS structure) with its aircraft detached to Topcliffe.

ZF135	ZF136	ZF137	ZF138	ZF139	ZF140	ZF143	ZF144	ZF160
ZF161	ZF162	ZF163	ZF164	ZF166	ZF168	ZF169	ZF200	ZF201
ZF203	ZF206	ZF207	ZF211	ZF212	ZF238	ZF241	ZF242	ZF263
ZF266	ZF268	ZF286	ZF288	ZF290	ZF292	ZF294	ZF295	ZF315
ZF318	ZF319	ZF320	ZF343	ZF345	ZF346	ZF348	ZF350	ZF372
ZF375	ZF376	ZF379	ZF380	ZF405	ZF406	ZF408	ZF410	ZF411
ZF412	ZF413	ZF414	ZF416	ZF417	ZF418	ZF445	ZF446	ZF447
ZF448	ZF449	ZF450	ZF483	ZF484	ZF485	ZF486	ZF487	ZF488
ZF489	ZF490	ZF492	ZF512	ZF513	ZF514	ZF515	ZF516	

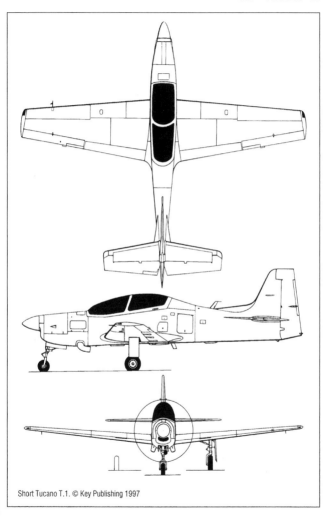

Short Tucano T.1. © Key Publishing 1997

VIGILANT T.1

Specification:
Powerplant: One Limbach L 2000 EB 1A piston engine of 80hp (59kW).
Performance: Max speed 149mph (240km/h).
Weights: Empty 1,278lb (580kg). Max take-off 1,818lb (825kg).
Dimensions: Span 54ft 5½in (16.60m). Length 25ft 7in (7.80m). Height 5ft 10¾in (1.80m).

Manufacturer: Burkhart Grob GmbH, Mattsies, Germany. Production complete.

Role & Variants: Two-seat powered sailplane for basic flying training and air experience flying. Manufacturer's designation G.109B.

First entered service: 1990.

Notes: See page 97 for integrated Volunteer Gliding School fleets. Illustrated below.

Colour scheme: White overall with red trim.

Volunteer Gliding School Gliders

Kestrel TX.1
Two-seat high performance sailplane built by Schempp-Hirth as the Janus. Illustrated in the foreground below. See page 97 for integrated Volunteer Gliding School fleets.

Valiant TX.1
Single-seat high performance standard class sailplane built by Schleicher as the AS-W 19B. See page 97 for integrated Volunteer Gliding School fleets.

Viking TX.1
Two-seat sailplane built by Grob as the G-103 Twin Astir. Illustrated in the background below. See page 97 for integrated Volunteer Gliding School fleets.

Volunteer Gliding Schools
Note that No.618 VGS is looking for a new home! All the gliders have been issued with a two-letter code to be worn on the wings and the fin.

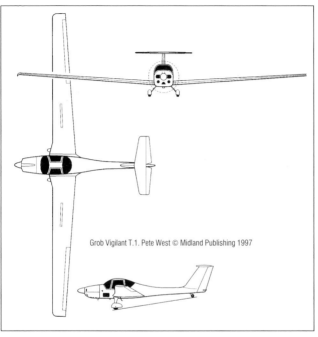

Grob Vigilant T.1. Pete West © Midland Publishing 1997

Central Gliding School
TA:ZH115   TF:ZH120   TJ:ZH123
UZ:ZH267   SB:ZH269   SC:ZH270
Viking   VD:ZE499   VE:ZE501
WB/ZE554   WD:ZE556   XJ:ZE609
Valiant   YW:ZD657   YX:ZD658

Vigilant T.1
TX:ZH185   UF:ZH193
Kestrel   SZ:ZD975
VM:ZE524   VP:ZE527
XR:ZE627   YB:ZE650
YY:ZD659   YZ:ZD660

RAF Syerston
UL:ZH205

VR:ZE529   VX:ZE550
YQ/ZE680

611 Volunteer Gliding School
VS/ZE530   VZ:ZE552   WA:ZE553

Viking TX.1
WS/ZE587   YL:ZE659

Watton (Army)

612 Volunteer Gliding School
TD:ZH118   UB:ZH189   UD:ZH191

Vigilant T.1
UJ:ZH196

Abingdon (Army)

613 Volunteer Gliding School
TU:ZH147   UG:ZH194   US:ZH247

Vigilant T.1
SD:ZH271

RAF Halton

614 Volunteer Gliding School
VJ/ZE520   VU:ZE532   VW:ZE534

Viking TX.1
VY/ZE551   XX:ZE633

Wethersfield
(MoD Police)

615 Volunteer Gliding School
WF/ZE558   WT:ZE590   WX:ZE594
YR/ZE681   **Kestrel**
SY/ZD974

Kestrel, Viking TX.1
XA:ZE601   XS:ZE628

RAF Kenley
YC/ZE651

616 Volunteer Gliding School
TH:ZH122   TQ:ZH129   TR:ZH144

Vigilant T.1
UU:ZH249   SA:ZH268

RAF Henlow

617 Volunteer Gliding School
VT/ZE531   XD:ZE604   XW:ZE632

Viking TX.1
YH:ZE656   YJ:ZE657

RAF Manston

621 Volunteer Gliding School
WJ/ZE561   XB:ZE602   XH:ZE608

Viking TX.1
YK:ZE658   YU:ZE684

Hullavington
(Army)

622 Volunteer Gliding School
VA/ZE495   VV:ZE533   WE:ZE557

Viking TX.1
WQ:ZE585   WY:ZE595

Upavon (Army)
WZ:ZE600   YA:ZE637

624 Volunteer Gliding School
TP:ZH128   TS:ZH145   TW:ZH184

Vigilant T.1

Chivenor (RM)

625 Volunteer Gliding School
WM/ZE564   XC:ZE603   XF:ZE606

Viking TX.1
XG:ZE607   XM:ZE613

Hullavington
XP:ZE625   **(Army)**

626 Volunteer Gliding School
VK:ZE521   WV:ZE592   XK:ZE610

Viking TX.1
XQ:ZE626

RNAS
Predannack

631 Volunteer Gliding School   **Viking TX.1**   **RAF Sealand**
WG/ZE559   WH/ZE560   WK/ZE562   WW/ZE593   XY/ZE635   YE/ZE653   YN/ZE678

632 Volunteer Gliding School   **Vigilant T.1**   **RAF Ternhill**
TC:ZH117   UC:ZH190   UN:ZH207   UV:ZH263

633 Volunteer Gliding School   **Vigilant T.1**   **RAF Cosford**
TG:ZH121   TL:ZH125   UM:ZH206   UX:ZH265   UY:ZH266

634 Volunteer Gliding School   **Viking TX.1**   **RAF St Athan**
VB/ZE496   VH/ZE504   VL/ZE522

635 Volunteer Gliding School   **Vigilant T.1**   **Samlesbury**
TE:ZH119   TY:ZH186   TZ:ZH187   UA:ZH188   UE:ZH192   **(BAe)**

636 Volunteer Gliding School   **Viking TX.1**   **DTEO Aberporth**
VN/ZE526   XL/ZE611   XZ/ZE636

637 Volunteer Gliding School   **Vigilant T.1**   **RAF Little**
TM:ZH126   TT:ZH146   TV:ZH148   **Rissington**

642 Volunteer Gliding School   **Vigilant T.1**   **RAF Linton-on**
TK:ZH124   TN:ZH127   UK:ZH197   UT:ZH248   UW:ZH264   **-Ouse**

643 Volunteer Gliding School   **Vigilant T.1**   **RAF Syerston**

644 Volunteer Gliding School   **Vigilant T.1**   **RAF Syerston**
Use Vigilants drawn from Central Gliding School pool.

645 Volunteer Gliding School   **Viking TX.1**   **Catterick (Army)**
VF/ZE502   VG/ZE503   VQ/ZE528   WC/ZE555   YS/ZE682   YT/ZE683

661 Volunteer Gliding School   **Viking TX.1**   **Kirknewton**
WL/ZE563   WP/ZE584   WR/ZE586   WU/ZE591   XN/ZE614   YV/ZE685   **(Army)**

662 Volunteer Gliding School   **Viking TX.1**   **Arbroath (RM)**
XE/ZE605   XT/ZE629   XU/ZE630   XV/ZE631   YP/ZE679

663 Volunteer Gliding School   **Vigilant T.1**   **RAF Kinloss**
UH:ZH195   UR:ZH211   SE:ZH890

664 Volunteer Gliding School   **Vigilant T.1**   **Belfast City**
TB:ZH116   UQ:ZH209   **Airport**

Battle of Britain Memorial Flight

RAF Coningsby

Douglas Dakota IV	YS-DM:ZA947	David Lord vc colours, illustrated below.
DHC Chipmunk T.10	WG486	conversion trainer.
DHC Chipmunk T.10	WK518	conversion trainer.
DH Devon C.2/2	VP981	in store.
Hawker Hurricane IIc	J:PZ865	Middle East colours, illustrated, bottom. (LF363 on rebuild.)
Avro Lancaster B.I	WS-J:PA474	9 Squadron colours, *Johnny Walker - Still Going Strong*.
V-S Spitfire IIa	RN-S:P7350	72 Squadron colours.
V-S Spitfire Vb	ZD-C:AB910	222 Squadron colours.
V-S Spitfire IX	21-V:MK356	433 Squadron colours.
V-S Spitfire PR.XIX	N:PM631	681 Squadron colours.
V-S Spitfire PR.XIX	PS915	2nd prototype Mk.XIV (JF319) colours.

FLEET AIR ARM

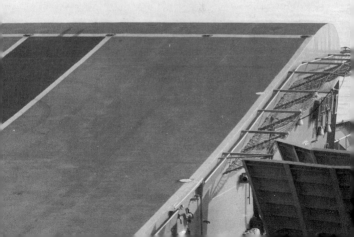

FLEET AIR ARM

Current organisation: numbers given at the end of column three denote references to the unit quoted in the main text.

NAVAL AIR COMMAND   HQ RNAS Yeovilton

RNAS Culdrose - HMS *Seahawk*, station code 'CU'

706 Squadron	Sea King HAS.5U	Anti-submarine training - 114
	Sea King HAS.6	
750 Squadron	Jetstream T.2	Observer training – 124
771 Squadron	Sea King HAR.5	Search and rescue training – 115
	Sea King HAS.5U	
810 Squadron	Sea King HAS.6	Anti-submarine warfare – 115
814 Squadron	Sea King HAS.6	Anti-submarine warfare, assigned to HMS *Invincible* – 116
820 Squadron	Sea King HAS.6	Anti-submarine warfare, assigned to HMS *Illustrious* – 117
849 Squadron	Sea King AEW.2	Airborne Early Warning – 119
Fleet Requirements & Direction Unit	Hawk T.1/T.1A	Civilian contracted unit – 121

RNAS Portland - HMS *Osprey*, station code 'PO'

702 Squadron	Lynx HAS.3	Ship's flight training – 110
815 Squadron	Lynx HAS.3	Ship's flight anti-surface/
	Lynx HMA8	anti-submarine – 112

(Portland will close in late 1997, with its units moving to Yeovilton.)

RNAS Prestwick - HMS *Gannet*, station code 'PW'

819 Squadron	Sea King HAS.6	Anti-submarine warfare, SAR – 116

RNAS Yeovilton - HMS *Heron*, station code 'VL'

800 Squadron	Sea Harrier FA2	Fighter, Ground attack/ reconnaissance, assigned to HMS *Invincible* – 102
801 Squadron	Sea Harrier FA2	Fighter/ground attack/ reconnaissance, assigned to HMS *Illustrious* – 104
845 Squadron	Sea King HC.4	Commando assault support – 117

(845 Squadron currently provides four Sea King HC.4s for the NATO IFOR Detachment in Split, Bosnia.)

846 Squadron	Sea King HC.4	Commando assault support – 118

847 Squadron	Gazelle AH.1	Royal Marines operations, 3 Commando Brigade – 108
	Lynx AH.7	Royal Marines operations, 3 Commando Brigade – 113
848 Squadron	Sea King HC.4	Commando assault support – 118
899 Squadron	Sea Harrier FA2	Fighter, ground attack/reconnaissance – 104
	Harrier T.4/T.8	Conversion training – 105
HMS *Heron* Station Flight	Jetstream T.3	Communications – 125
Flag Officer Naval Aviation	Gazelle HT.2	Communications – 108
RN Historic Flight	Various	Display aircraft – 126

Civilian Contract Flying, not listed above

| Bond Helicopters, Roborough | Dauphin | Communications and other duties for Flag Officer Training – 106 |
| Defence Helicopter Flying School, Shawbury | Squirrel HT.1 | Initial pilot training, tri-service unit – 58, 120, 140 |

(No.705 Squadron is 'shadow' unit for the Navy side of operations.)

FR Aviation, Bournemouth and elsewhere	Falcon 20	Fleet target facilities – 80, 120
Joint Elementary Flying Training School, Barkston Heath	Firefly	Initial pilot training, tri-service unit – 82
Naval Flying Grading Flight, Roborough	Grob G.115	Initial pilot grading – 122

See also under 32 (The Royal) Squadron, RAF – page 39. The HS.125 element of the Squadron includes Fleet Air Arm pilots on strength and undertakes some taskings for the Navy.

SEA HARRIER FA2, T.8

Specification (F/A.2):

Powerplant: One Rolls-Royce Pegasus Mk.104 vectored thrust turbofan of 21,500lb st (95.6kN) dry.

Performance: Max speed ('clean') approx 736mph (1,185km/h) at sea level. Typical combat radius 230 miles (370km).

Weights: Empty approx 13,000lb (5,897kg). Max take-off 26,200lb (11,884kg).

Dimensions: Span 25ft 3in (7.70m). Length 46ft 6in (14.17m). Height 12ft 2in (3.71m).

Armament: Max ordnance load 8,000lb (3,629kg). Four wing and two under fuselage hardpoints. Provision for bombs, rocket pods, AIM-120 AMRAAM air-to-air missiles. Limited reconnaissance capability.

Manufacturer: British Aerospace, Dunsfold, Surrey and Brough, Yorks. Production and upgrading continuing.

Roles & Variants: Single-seat vertical/short take-off and landing (V/STOL) point defence, ground attack and reconnaissance (FA2) and two-seat conversion trainer (T.8). Single-seaters initially designated FRS.2, later adopting FA2. Note lack of full stop between role designator and mark number, a trend that has continued with the Merlin – see page 148. Some elements of the Navy quote the Sea Harrier as the F/A2 (ie shades of the US McDD F/A-18 Hornet) but the majority seems to go for FA2! T.8 originally referred to as the T.8N, but this suffix now appears to be not used. Conversions from original FRS.1 (illustrated on page 99) and new-build airframes in the programme.

First entered service: 1993 (FRS.2)

Colour scheme: Overall tactical grey colour scheme for F/A.2s, two-seaters overall gloss black.

See also: RAF operates the Harrier GR.7 and T.10 (see page 8) see also 'Test & Trials' (page 143).

---

800 Squadron   Sea Harrier F/A2   Yeovilton

Black winged swords against a black trident, not recently observed on aircraft. Aircraft codes in white on forward nozzle coaming. Assigned to HMS *Invincible* (deck code 'N').

122:ZH798   123:ZD607   124:ZH800   125:ZA175   126:ZE696   127:ZH805

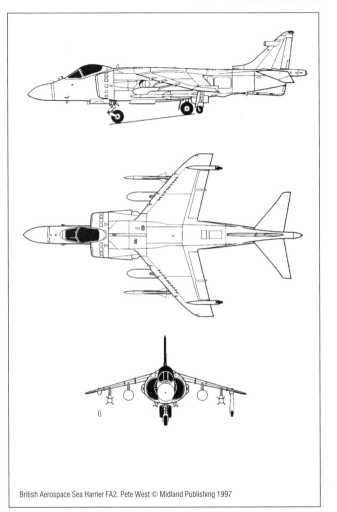

British Aerospace Sea Harrier FA2. Pete West © Midland Publishing 1997

801 Squadron   Sea Harrier FA2   Yeovilton

Black winged trident, not recently observed on aircraft. Aircraft codes in white on forward nozzle coaming, station code 'VL'. Assigned to HMS *Illustrious*.

000:ZD578   001:ZE693   002:ZH802   003:ZE697   004:ZH799   005:ZD614

899 Squadron   FA2, T.8* Yeovilton

Black mailed fist, not recently observed on aircraft. Aircraft codes in white on forward nozzle coaming.

710:ZE690   711:ZE692   712:ZD582   714:XZ459   715:ZH796   716:ZH797
717:ZD608   718:ZE695   719:ZD612   720:ZB605*   721:ZD990*   723:ZD993*
724:ZD992*

The Fleet Air Arm's two-seater Harriers – all serving with 899 Squadron – wear overall overall gloss black 'high visibility' colours.

Development Sea Harrier FA2 (initially designated FRS.2) taking the training 'ski-jump' at RNAS Yeovilton.

DAUPHIN

Specification:
Powerplant: Two Turboméca Arriel 1C1 turboshafts each of 724shp (540kW).
Performance: Max speed 176mph (283km/h). Range 530 miles (852km).
Weights: Empty 4,764lb (2,161kg). Max take-off 9,039lb (4,100kg).
Dimensions: Rotor diameter 39ft 2in (11.94m). Length 38ft 9½in (11.63m). Height 11ft 6½in (3.52m).

Manufacturer: Aérospatiale (now Eurocopter) Marignane, France. Production continuing.

Role & Variants: Nine seat general purpose twin turbine helicopter. (Dauphin = Dolphin.) Manufacturer's designation SA.365N (with Eurocopter AS.365N).

First entered service: 1996 (Fleet Air Arm contract)

Notes: Contractor owned and operated on behalf of Flag Officer Training.

Colour scheme: Overall gloss ruby red with white 'Royal Navy' and 'Bond' logo. Red/white/blue roundel.

Bond Helicopters   Dauphin SA.365N   Roborough
ZJ164   ZJ165

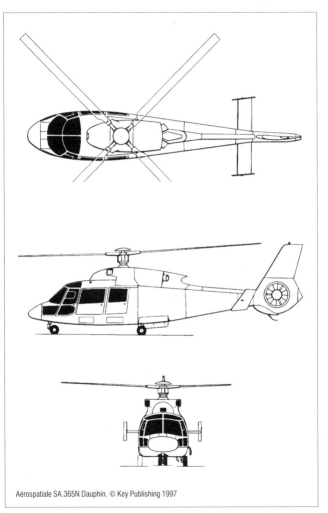

Aérospatiale SA.365N Dauphin. © Key Publishing 1997

GAZELLE AH.1 and HT.2

Specification (HT.2):
Powerplant: One Turboméca Astazou IIIN turboshaft of 592shp (441kW).
Performance: Max speed 193mph (310km/h) at sea level. Range 416 miles (670km).
Weights: Empty 2,028lb (920kg). Max take-off 3,968lb (1,800kg).
Dimensions: Rotor diameter 34ft 5½in (10.50m). Length 31ft 3in (9.52m). Height 8ft 11in (2.72m).

Manufacturer: Sud Aviation/Aérospatiale (now Eurocopter) Marignane, France with co-production and assembly by Westland Helicopters, Yeovil, Somerset, UK. Production complete.

Roles & Variants: Five-seat observation and light transport (AH.1) and basic trainer and light transport (HT.2) helicopter. Manufacturer's designation SA.341B (AH.1) and SA.341C (HT.2).

First entered service: 1973 (HT.2).

Notes: With the disbanding of 705 Squadron on Gazelle HT.2s at Culdrose in March 1997 (the 'number plate' being taken up by the Navy element of the DHFS, see page 120) a large number of HT.2s will be placed in store pending disposal, some may well go to the RAF as instructional airframes. Some remain in use as 'hacks', see below.

Colour scheme: Grey/green overall camouflage (AH.1) and white with red stripe (HT.2).

See also: Army Air Corps also operates the Gazelle AH.1 extensively, see page 133. See also 'Test & Trials' (page 143).

847 Squadron	Gazelle AH.1	Yeovilton

Single-letter aircraft code in black on the fin. Illustrated below. Unit also operates the Lynx AH.7 (see page 110).
A:XX380   B:XX412   C:ZB676   D:XX450   E:ZA728   G:XW849   H:XW851

Flag Officer Naval Aviation	Gazelle HT.2	Yeovilton

Station code 'VL' on tail.
ZB649

Naval Aircraft Repair Organisation	Gazelle HT.2	Fleetlands

Station code 'FL' on tail.
XW887

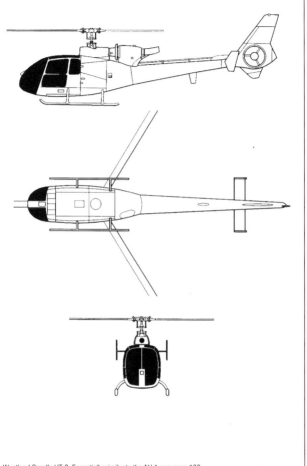

Westland Gazelle HT.2. Essentially similar to the AH.1, see page 133.
Pete West © Midland Publishing 1997

LYNX HAS.3, AH.7 and HMA8

Specification (HMA8):

Powerplant: Two Rolls-Royce Gem 42-1 turboshafts each of 1,135shp (846kW).

Performance: Max speed 144mph (232km/h). Typical combat radius 170 miles (274km).

Weights: Empty 7,255lb (3,291kg). Max take-off 11,300lb (5,126kg).

Dimensions: Rotor diameter 42ft 0in (12.80m). Length 39ft 2in (11.92m). Height 12ft 0½in (3.67m).

Armament: Four Sea Skua air-to-surface missiles, sophisticated detection and self-defence suite.

Manufacturer: Westland Helicopters, Yeovil (with Aérospatiale – now Eurocopter – as sub-contractor). Production for Fleet Air Arm complete, upgrades to HMA8 continuing. Production of the Super Lynx for export continuing.

Roles & Variants: Shipboard anti-submarine and anti-surface vessel (HAS.3 and HMA8) and general purpose battlefield transport (AH.7) helicopter – more details of the latter on page 136. HAS.3 (illustrated opposite) an upgraded version of the original

Fleet Air Arm HAS.2 (plus new-build order) and currently operating with the following sub-variants: HAS.3S with enhanced systems; HAS.3S(ICE) less sophisticated version used on the Antarctic patrol and survey vessel HMS *Endurance*; HAS.3SGM modified for use in the Arabian Gulf with improved cooling, infra-red and electronic countermeasures. HAS.3CTS with improved tactical attack system now effectively out of use, having been upgraded to HMA8 standards. HMA8 (note lack of full stop between role designator and mark number) was originally known as the HAS.8 and features a considerable upgrade in performance and facilities, including the new BERP (British Experimental Rotor Programme) main rotor blades and enhanced communications and tactical systems.

First entered service: 1982 (HAS.3).

Colour scheme: Overall maritime light grey (HAS.3 and HMA8) with bright red patches on the *Endurance* examples and large Union Flags on the Gulf Patrol versions. Grey/green overall camouflage on AH.7s.

See also: Army Air Corps also operates the Lynx extensively, see page 136. See also 'Test & Trials' (page 143).

702 Squadron   Lynx HAS.3S   Portland

Some aircraft carry a small Lynx's head on the engine cowls. No.702 Squadron will move to Yeovilton when Portland closes during the latter half of 1997.

630:ZD565   631:ZD251   632:XZ729   633:ZD258   634:XZ248   635:ZX235
636:ZD263   642:ZD249   644:XZ719   645:ZD254

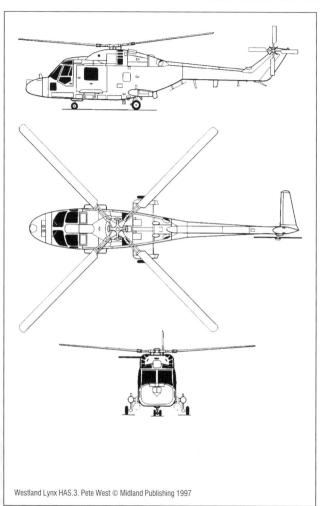

Westland Lynx HAS.3. Pete West © Midland Publishing 1997

815 Squadron   Lynx HAS.3, HMA8   Portland

Some aircraft have a harp logo, others an owl (reflecting previous and existing 'sponsors', Guinness and Guardian Royal. Some carry individual names and/or nose-art. The unit is responsible for providing all Ships' Flights with Lynx helicopters and crews, include the HMA8 Operational Evaluation Unit (OEU). No.815 Squadron will eventually move to Yeovilton when Portland closes (expected to be later in 1997).

Headquarters Flight & HMA8 OEU Lynx HAS.3S, HAS.3SGM+, HMA.8*

Three-figure codes in white on the main doors.

301:XZ693 302:XZ726 303:XZ699 304:XZ730 306:XZ245+ 307:XZ721+
308:XZ698+ 670:XZ732* 671:ZD252* 672:ZD261* 673:ZF558*

Ships' Flights   Lynx HAS.3S, HAS.3SGM+, HAS.3S(ICE)°, HMA8*

Three figure codes in white on the main door. Two-letter deck code on the rotor pylon (given after the name of the Ships' Flight below).

328	XZ724+	*Brave*, 'BA'		405	XZ250	*London*, 'LO'
332	XZ727	*Liverpool*, 'LP'		407	XZ228+	*York*, 'YK'
333	ZD259	*Birmingham*, 'BM'		410	ZD253+	— 'GC'
334	XZ229+	— 'SN'		411	XZ239+	*Edinburgh*, 'EB'
336	XZ254	*Coventry*, 'CV'		415	ZF563*	*Monmouth*, 'MM'
338	XZ725	*Campletown*, 'CT'		417	XZ694	*Nottingham*, 'NM'
345	XZ695	*Newcastle*, 'NC'		420	ZD264+	*Exeter*, 'EX'
355	XZ257	— 'SM'		422	XZ256	— 'SU'
361	XZ234	*Norfolk*, 'NF'		434	XZ238°	*Endurance*, 'ED'
365	XZ722*	*Argyll*, 'AY'		435	XZ246°	*Endurance*, 'ED'
372	ZD265*	*Northumberland*, 'NL'		444	ZF557*	*Montrose*, 'MR'
374	ZD255+	*Beaver*, 'VB'		457	ZF562*	*Lancaster*, 'LA'
376	XZ736	*Boxer*, 'XB'		462	XZ690	*Westminster*, 'WM'
404	ZF560*	*Iron Duke*, 'IR'		474	XZ691*	*Richmond*, 'RM'
				479	XZ696+	—

Below, left: No.815 Squadron HAS.3S. Above: No.815 Squadron HMA8.

847 Squadron   **AH.7**   **Yeovilton**

Single-letter code in black underneath the cockpit. Also operate the Gazelle AH.1
see page 108).

L:ZD282   N:XZ612   R:XZ180   X:XZ614   Y:XZ605

SEA KING AEW.2A, AEW.7, HAR/HAS.5, HAS.6, COMMANDO HC.4

Specification (HAS.6):

Powerplant: Two Rolls-Royce Gnome H.1400-1T turboshafts each of 1,660shp (1,238kW).

Performance: Max speed 140mph (226km/h) at sea level. Ferry range 1,082 miles (1,742km).

Weights: Empty 11,891lb (5,393kg). Max take-off 21,500lb (9,752kg).

Dimensions: Main rotor 62ft 0in (18.90m). Length 55ft 10in (17.02m). Height 15ft 11in (4.85m).

Armament: Maximum ordnance 2,500lb (1,134kg) including up to four torpedoes or depth charges carried externally. Door-mounted 7.62mm machine can be fitting in Sea King or Commando HC.4.

Manufacturer: Westland Helicopters Ltd, Yeovil, Somerset. Production for the Fleet Air Arm completed. Conversions and upgrades underway.

Roles & Variants: Large twin-turbine, amphibious, shipborne helicopter with the following major variants: AEW.2A airborne early warning with large radar mounted on the starboard side, upgrade to AEW.7 status underway; HAR.5 long range search and rescue; HAS.5(U) general purpose utility; HAS.6 all weather anti-submarine warfare. Note that the HAS.5(U) may be designated HU.5, but this is not confirmed. Mk.5 and Mk.6 upgrades from the previous HAS.2 standard plus new-builds. Commando HC.4, large twin-turbine, non-amphibious, shipborne troop transport and assault helicopter. Highly developed, licence produced derivative of the Sikorsky SH-3D Sea King (Model S-61).

First entered service: 1980 (HAS.5 and Commando HC.4), 1982 (AEW.2A).

Colour scheme: Overall dark maritime grey, SAR examples with large red panels. Special camouflages for IFOR-assigned aircraft.

See also: RAF also operates the Sea King, see page 62. See also page 63 for three-view illustration, essentially similar in format to the Naval versions. See also 'Trials and Test' (page 143).

---

706 Squadron   Sea King HAS.5(U)*, HAS.6   Culdrose

Three-digit codes in white below cockpit, with 'last two' repeated on rear fuselage and nose. Station code 'CU'.

581:ZA166*   583:XV706   585:XV709   587:XZ921   588:XV670*   592:ZA127
597:XV673*   598:XV675   599:XV651*

771 Squadron   **Sea King HAR.5, HAS.5(U)***   **Culdrose**
Three-digit codes in white below cockpit, with 'last two' repeated on rear fuselage and nose.
Ace of Spades card behind cockpit.
820:XV647   821:XV705   822:XZ920   823:XV666   824:ZA134*   825:ZA167*

810 Squadron   **Sea King HAS.6**   **Culdrose**
Three-digit codes in white below cockpit, with 'last two' repeated on rear fuselage and nose.
500:XV653   501:XV708   502:ZA129   503:XZ922   504:ZG817   505:XV665
506:ZD634   508:XV700   509:ZA126   510:XV659   511:XV660   515:XV676

814 Squadron   Sea King HAS.6   Culdrose

Three-digit codes in white below cockpit, with 'last two' repeated on rear fuselage and nose. Assigned to HMS *Invincible* (deck code 'N').

265:ZA169   266:XV712   267:XV655   268:XV701   269:XZ581   270:ZG819
271:ZA131

819 Squadron   Sea King HAS.5(U)*, HAS.6   Prestwick

Three-digit codes in white below cockpit, with 'last two' repeated on rear fuselage and nose. Scottish flag (white cross on dark blue background) in circle near cockpit on some aircraft.Station code 'PW'.

700:ZD637   701:ZG816   702:ZG875   703:XV643   704:XZ580   705:XV674
706:XZ579   707:ZG818   708:XV696   709:XV711   826:XV699*

820 Squadron   Sea King HAS.6   Culdrose

Three-digit codes in white below cockpit, with 'last two' repeated on rear fuselage and nose. Assigned to HMS *Illustrious* (deck code 'L').

010:ZA135 011:XV703 012:XV710 013:ZA128 014:XZ571 015:XZ574
018:XV713

845 Squadron   Commando HC.4   Yeovilton

Single-letter codes carried in black on the fuselage side and nose. No.845 Squadron currently provides four Sea King HC.4s for the NATO IFOR Detachment in Split, Bosnia.

A:ZG820 B:ZE427 C:ZA297 D:ZG821 E:ZD480 F:ZA314
G:ZA298 H:ZD477 J:ZE425 K:ZF120 L:ZF124 M:ZA313

846 Squadron　　　Commando HC.4　　　Yeovilton

Two-letter codes in black on the fuselage side.

VF:ZD625	VG:ZD478	VH:ZF119	VI:ZF122	VJ:ZF121	VK:ZE428	VL:ZD627
VM:ZA295	VN:ZG822	VO:ZA296	VP:ZF118	VQ:ZF117		

848 Squadron　　　Commando HC.4　　　Yeovilton

Two-letter codes in black on the fuselage side.

ZO:ZA293	ZP:ZF116	ZQ:ZF123	ZR:ZA292	ZS:ZA312	ZT:ZA299	ZU:ZD476
ZV:ZD479	ZW:ZE426	ZY:ZA310	ZZ:ZD626			

849 Squadron   Sea King AEW.2A, HAS.5(U)*   Culdrose

Three-digit codes in white below cockpit, with 'last two' repeated on rear fuselage and nose. No.849 has an HQ Flight plus two Ships' Flights, 'A' Flight which is assigned to HMS *Invincible* (deck code 'N') and 'B' Flight assigned to HMS *Illustrious* (deck code 'L'). Sea King AEW.7 conversions underway for this unit. Illustrated above and below.

180:XV656   182:XV672   183:XV697   184:XV650   185:XV671   186:XV649
187:XV714   188:XZ578*

SQUIRREL HT.1

Specification: See page 140.

Manufacturer: Eurocopter, Marignane, France. Deliveries to DHFS due to be completed 1997, production for other customers continuing.

Roles & Variants: Training helicopter. Manufacturer's designation AS.350B and known as the Ecureuil (= Squirrel) in France and the A-Star in the USA.

First entered service: 1997.

Notes: Operated within the Defence Helicopter Flying School (run by FBS Ltd, a combined operation by FR Aviation, Bristow Helicopters and SERCO) to train helicopter pilots for all three services. DHFS officially came into operation at Shawbury, Shropshire, in 1st April 1997.

Colour scheme: Gloss black fuselage with gloss yellow engine bay.

See also: Main entry for the Squirrel HT.1/HT.2 on page 140. The RAF also operates the essentially similar Twin Squirrel, see page 68 for details and the broadly similar three-view.

705 Squadron   Squirrel HT.1   DHFS Shawbury

With the disbanding of 705 Squadron on Gazelle HT.2s (see page 108) at Culdrose in March 1997, the 'number plate' was taken up by the Navy element of the DHFS with 705 thought to be nominally in charge of the advanced training syllabus. See page 140 for the Squirrel fleet. However, as *Air Forces UK* went to press, 705 were still operating Gazelles out of Culdrose, probably as 'hand-over' support.

FALCON 20C, 'DC and 'E

Roles & Variants: Twin-jet weapons and system facilities trainer. For further technical details refer to page 80.

Notes: Contractor owned and operated by FR Aviation, based at Bournemouth and operating since 1986 under contract to the Royal Navy for a variety of simulated threat/countermeasures and target facilities training. FR Aviation also operates Cessna 441 Conquest IIs G-FRAX and G-FRAZ and Beech E55 Baron G-FRBY which are occasionally used by the Royal Navy. More details of the Falcon fleet appear on page 80.

HAWK T.1, T.1A

Roles & Variants: Two-seat target facilities and gun laying systems trainer. For full technical details and three-view illustration refer to the RAF entry for the Hawk on page 84.

First entered service: 1994.

Colour scheme: Overall gloss black.

See also: The RAF widely operates the Hawk, see page 80. See also 'Test & Trials' (page 143).

Fleet Requirements & Direction Unit   Hawk T.1/T.1A*   Culdrose

Some letter codes survive from previous RAF units, these are being removed on respray. Winged FRADU crest on the fin. 'Royal Navy' in white on the rear fuselage.

XX157*	XX175	XX183	XX201*	XX205*	XX217*	DV:XX234
Y:XX242	XX245	XX263*	DK:XX286*	XX301*	XX311	
DA:XX315*	W:XX322*	XX337*	XX346*			

HERON

Specification:
Powerplant: One Textron Lycoming O-320-E2A piston engine of 150hp (112kW).
Performance: Max speed 155mph (250km/h). Range 453 miles (730km).
Weights: Empty 1,565lb (710kg). Max take-off 2,641lb (1,198kg).
Dimensions: Span 32ft 9½in (10.00m). Length 24ft 1¾in (7.36m). Height 9ft 3in (2.82m).

Manufacturer: Burkhart Grob, Mindelheim, Germany. Production of Herons completed.

Role & Variants: Two-seat basic trainer. Manufacturer's designation G 115D-2.

First entered service: 1994.

Notes: Contractor owned and operated, by Shorts Support Services for the Fleet Air Arm. Civilian registered.

Colour scheme: White with two-tone blue trim.

See also: Page 74.

Naval Flying Grading Flight   Heron   Roborough
G-BVHC   G-BVHD   G-BVHE   G-BVHF   G-BVHG

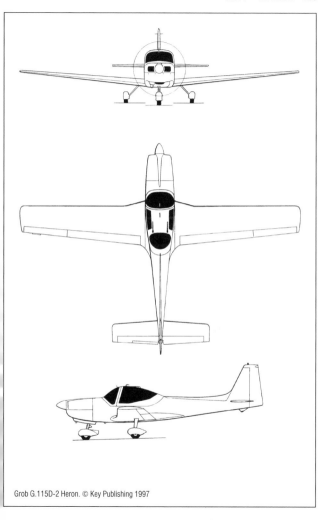

Grob G.115D-2 Heron. © Key Publishing 1997

JETSTREAM T.2, T.3

Specification (T.3):
(See page 90 for the T.2 specification, which is generally similar to the RAF's T.1.)
Powerplant: Two Garrett TPE331-10UG turboprops each of 940shp (701kW).
Performance: Max speed 303mph (488km/h) at 15,000ft (4,570m). 783 miles (1,260km).
Weights: Empty 9,894lb (4,488kg). Max take-off 15,322lb (6,950kg).
Dimensions: Span 52ft 0in (15.85m). Length 47ft 1½in (14.37m). Height 17ft 8in (5.38m).

Manufacturer: Scottish Aviation (now British Aerospace), Prestwick, Scotland (T.2). British Aerospace (now AI[R]), Prestwick, Scotland (T.3). Production completed.

Roles & Variants: Twin-turboprop observer trainer (T.2) and helicopter observer trainer (T.3) both with reserve transport capability. T.3 fitted with Racal ASR.360 radar under the wing centre section. Initial manufacturer's designation HP.137. T.3 civilian equivalent Jetstream 31.

First entered service: 1978 (T.2), 1986 (T.3).

Colour scheme: White upper fuselage, blue cheat line, light grey under surfaces and wings.

See also: Page 90 for details of the RAF T.1 and for a three-view illustration which is generally very similar for the T.2 and of the same layout for the T.3. See also 'Test & Trials' (page 143).

750 Squadron   Jetstream T.2   Culdrose

Three-digit code in white under cockpit, with 'last two' repeated on rudder. Station code 'CU'.
560:XX481   561:XX476   562:XX488   563:ZA110   564:XX478   565:ZA111
566:XX484   567:XX485   568:XX487   569:XX486   570:XX490

HMS *Heron* Station Flight   Jetstream T.3   Yeovilton
Three-digit code in white under cockpit, with 'last two' repeated on rudder.
576:ZE438   577:ZE439   578:ZE440   579:ZE441

HISTORIC

Royal Navy Historic Flight   Yeovilton

The Flight is now a civilian charitable trust, entitled the Swordfish Trust. One of the Swordfish is now civilian registered, although the registration is not worn on the airframe.

Chipmunk T.10	908:WB657	conversion trainer
Chipmunk T.10	906:WK608	conversion trainer
Firefly AS.5	204:WB271	under restoration
Sea Fury FB.11	VR930	—
Sea Hawk FGA.6	188:WV908	—
Swordfish II	A2A:W5856	G-BMGC, 810 Squadron colours – see below
Swordfish II	L2:LS326	836 Squadron colours

ARMY AIR CORPS

ARMY AIR CORPS

Current organisation: numbers given in column three refer the rear to the entry in the main text. Army Air Corps structure is based on a series of Regiments, within which are a number of Squadrons or Flights.

HQ Director Army Aviation   **Middle Wallop**

667 (Development & Trials)Squadron	Middle Wallop	Gazelle AH.1 - 134 Lynx AH.7 – 139

1 Regiment AAC   **Gütersloh, Germany**

651 Squadron	Gütersloh	Gazelle AH.1 – 133, Lynx AH.7 – 138
652 Squadron	Gütersloh	Gazelle AH.1 – 133, Lynx AH.7 – 138
661 Squadron	Gütersloh	Gazelle AH.1 – 134, Lynx AH.7 – 138

2 (Training Regiment) AAC   **Middle Wallop**

Joint Elementary Flying Training Squadron	RAF Barkston Heath	Firefly tri-service unit – 82
Defence Helicopter Flying School	RAF Shawbury (660 Squadron)	Squirrel HT.1 tri-service unit – 140
Advanced Fixed Wing Flight	Middle Wallop	Islander AL.1 – 141
670 (Operational Training) Squadron	Middle Wallop	Gazelle AH.1 – 134 Squirrel HT.2 – 140
671 (Operational Conversion) Squadron	Middle Wallop	Gazelle AH.1 – 134, Lynx AH.7 – 139

3 Regiment AAC   **Wattisham**

653 Squadron	Wattisham	Lynx AH.9 – 138
662 Squadron	Wattisham	Gazelle AH.1 – 134, Lynx AH.7 – 138
663 Squadron	Wattisham	Gazelle AH.1 – 134, Lynx AH.7 – 139

4 Regiment AAC   **Wattisham**

654 Squadron	Wattisham	Gazelle AH.1 – 133, Lynx AH.7 – 138
659 Squadron	Wattisham	Lynx AH.9 – 138
669 Squadron	Wattisham	Gazelle AH.1 – 134, Lynx AH.7 – 139

5 Regiment   **Aldergrove**

655 Squadron	Aldergrove	Lynx AH.7 – 138
665 Squadron	Aldergrove	Gazelle AH.1 – 134
1 Flight	Aldergrove	Islander AL.1 – 141

7 Regiment AAC (Volunteers) Netheravon

658 Squadron (Volunteers)	Netheravon	Gazelle AH.1 – 133
666 Squadron (Volunteers)	Netheravon	Gazelle AH.1 – 134
3 Flight (Volunteers)	RAF Leuchars	Gazelle AH.1 – 134
6 Flight (Volunteers)	RAF Shawbury	Gazelle AH.1 – 135

9 Regiment AAC Dishforth

656 Squadron	Dishforth	Gazelle AH.1 – 133, Lynx AH.7 – 138
657 Squadron	Dishforth	Gazelle AH.1 – 133, Lynx AH.7 – 138
664 Squadron	Dishforth	Gazelle AH.1 – 134, Lynx AH.7 – 139

Independent Flights

7 Flight	Brunei	Bell 212 – 132
8 Flight	Hereford	Agusta A.109A – 130
		Gazelle AH.1 – 135
12 Flight	RAF Brüggen, Germany	Gazelle AH.1 – 135
16 Flight	Dhekelia, Cyprus	Gazelle AH.1 – 135
25 Flight	Belize	Gazelle AH.1 – 135, Lynx AH.7 – 139
AAC Flight BATU	Suffield, Canada	Gazelle AH.1 – 135
SFOR Bosnia	Gornji Vakuf, Bosnia	Gazelle AH.1, Lynx AH.7.

No.662 Squadron Gazelle AH.1, part of No.3 Regiment, and based at Wattisham.

AGUSTA A.109A

....

Specification:
Powerplant: Two Allison 250-C20B turboshafts of 420shp (313kW).
Performance: Maximum speed 193mph (311km/h). Range, with no reserves 351 miles (565km).
Weights: Empty 3,120lb (1,415kg). Max take-off 5,732lb (2,600kg).
Dimensions: Rotor diameter 36ft 1in (11.00m). Length 35ft 1½in (10.7m). Height 10ft 10in (3.3m).

Manufacturer: Agusta SpA, Cascina Costa, Italy. Production of A.109A completed, various versions still in production. The initial civil variant (A 109C) was known as the Hirundo (Swallow) but this name was quickly dropped.

Role & Variants: Eight seat general purpose helicopter, used primarily for special forces support.

First entered service: 1982.

Notes: First two aircraft captured during the Falklands conflict, having been previously operated by the Argentine Army. Two additional examples bought from new. Essentially operate as the air arm of 22 (Special Air Service) Regiment on communications and other duties within the UK.

Colour Scheme: Very 'civilian' in appearance (essentially white overall with blue cheat-lines. No roundels worn, military serial number only.

8 Flight   Agusta A.109A   Hereford
The Flight also operates Gazelle AH.1s, see page 135.
ZE410   ZE411   ZE412   ZE413

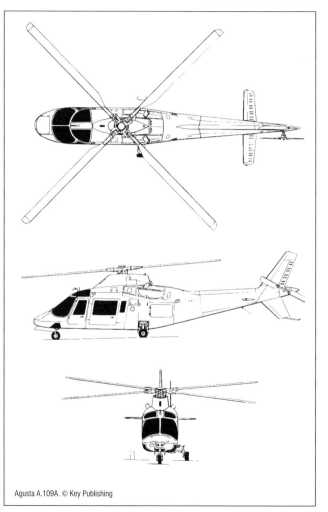

Agusta A.109A. © Key Publishing

BELL 212

Specification:
Powerplant: One Pratt & Whitney Canada T400-CP-400 TwinPac coupled turboshaft of 1,800shp (1,342kW).
Performance: Maximum speed 161mph (259km/h). Range 261 miles (420km).
Weights: Empty 6,143lb (2,787kg). Max take-off 11,200lb (5,080kg).
Dimensions: Rotor diameter 48ft 2¼in (14.69m). Length 42ft 4¾in (12.92m). Height 14ft 10¼in (4.53m).

Manufacturer: Bell Helicopter Textron, Fort Worth, Texas, USA. Production completed. US equivalent designation UH-1N Iroquois, civilian name Twin Two-Twelve.

Role & Variants: Medium transport helicopter.

First entered service: 1995.

Notes: Used for training and exercises in Brunei – local forces similarly equipped.

Colour scheme: Overall dark green/grey camouflage.

See also: Defence Helicopter Flying School at Shawbury operates the essentially similar Bell 412EP Griffin HT.1, see pages 58/59 for other details and three-view illustration.

7 Flight		**Bell 212**	**Brunei**
See above.			
ZH814	ZH815	ZH816	

GAZELLE AH.1

Specification:

Powerplant: One Turboméca Astazou IIIN turboshaft of 592shp (441kW).

Performance: Max speed 193mph (310km/h) at sea level. Range 416 miles (670km).

Weights: Empty 2,028lb (920kg). Max take-off 3,968lb (1,800kg).

Dimensions: Rotor diameter 34ft 5½in (10.50m). Length 31ft 3in (9.52m). Height 8ft 11in (2.72m).

Manufacturer: Sud Aviation/Aérospatiale (now Eurocopter) Marignane, France with co-production and assembly by Westland Helicopters, Yeovil, Somerset, UK. Production complete.

Roles & Variants: Five-seat observation and light transport helicopter.

First entered service: 1973.

Notes: Because 9 Regiment are currently providing helicopters for the SFOR detachment in Bosnia there is considerable interchange between squadrons (aircrews are currently being provided by 4 Regiment at Wattisham).

Colour scheme: Grey/green overall camouflage.

See also: Royal Marines also the Gazelle AH.1 and the Fleet Air Arm operates limited numbers of HT.2s, see page 108. See page 109 for three-view illustration. See also 'Test & Trials' (page 143).

651 Squadron   **Gazelle AH.1**   **Gütersloh, Germany**
Unit also operates the Lynx AH.7, see page 136.
XW844   XX418   ZA766

652 Squadron   **Gazelle AH.1**   **Gütersloh, Germany**
Unit also operates the Lynx AH.7, see page 136.
XX384   XX437   XX455

654 Squadron   **Gazelle AH.1**   **Wattisham**
Unit also operates the Lynx AH.7, see page 136.
XX460   XZ296   XZ328

656 Squadron   **Gazelle AH.1**   **Dishforth**
Unit also operates the Lynx AH.7, see page 136.
XW885   XW909   XX389   XZ298   XZ337   XZ347

657 Squadron   **Gazelle AH.1**   **Dishforth**
Single-letter codes in black on fuselage sides. Unit also operates the Lynx AH.7, see page 136.
XX372   XX438   XZ308

658 Squadron (V)   **Gazelle AH.1**   **Netheravon**
Single-letter codes in black on fuselage sides. Incorporates 2 Flight. See page 135.
T:XX445   V:ZA729   W:XX462   X:XZ294   Y:XX443   Z:XW899

661 Squadron   Gazelle AH.1   Gütersloh, Germany

Unit also operates the Lynx AH.7, see page 136.

XX395	XX414	XZ342	XZ343

662 Squadron   Gazelle AH.1   Wattisham

Single-letter codes in black on fuselage sides. Unit also operates the Lynx AH.7, see page 136.

U:XZ301	W:XX454	X:XX419	Y:XW913	XX439	XX449

663 Squadron   Gazelle AH.1   Wattisham

Single-letter or single-digit codes in black on fuselage sides. Unit also operates the Lynx AH.7, see page 136.

A:XZ313	B:XZ331	2:XX453	3:XZ292	XX444	ZB672

664 Squadron   Gazelle AH.1   Dishforth

Unit also operates the Lynx AH.7, see page 136.

XX381	XX399	XX448	XZ312	XZ338	ZA771

665 Squadron   Gazelle AH.1   Aldergrove

XW847	XW893	XX370	XX432	XZ299	XZ321	XZ346
ZA730	ZA772	ZA774	ZA775	ZB665	ZB670	ZB674
ZB682	ZB683	ZB684	ZB685	ZB686		

666 Squadron (V)   Gazelle AH.1   Netheravon

Single-letter codes in black on fuselage sides.

B:XZ316	C:XW892	D:XX383	E:XX442	F:ZA773	H:XW911

667 Squadron   Gazelle AH.1   Middle Wallop

Unit also operates the Lynx AH.7, see page 136.

XX417	XZ339

669 Squadron   Gazelle AH.1   Wattisham

Unit also operates the Lynx AH.7, see page 136.

XX394	XX409	XZ320	XZ345	ZB669

670 Squadron   Gazelle AH.1   Middle Wallop

Single-letter and single-letter, single-number codes in black. Unit also will operate the Squirrel HT.2 from September 1997, see page 140. Upon receipt of the Squirrels, some Gazelles will go to 671 Squadron.

A:XZ333	B:ZA777	C:XW865	D:XW848	E:XW908	F:XZ290	G:ZB666
H:ZB688	I:XZ344	J:XZ329	K:ZA769	L:XZ300	M:XW846	N:XZ322
O:XZ332	P:ZB673	Q:XX378	R:XZ317	S:XZ334	T:XZ325	U:XX403
V:ZA737	W:XX435	X:XX385	Y:XZ330	Z:XW897	A1:XX392	B1:XZ327
C1:XX405	D1:XX447	E1:XX375	F1:XZ344	G1:XZ349	H1:XW904	

671 Squadron   Middle Wallop
Some Gazelle AH.1s are to be transferred from 670 Squadron (see page 134) with its re-equipment with Squirrel HT.2s (see page 140). Unit also operates the Lynx AH.7, see page 136.

3 Flight (V)   Gazelle AH.1   RAF Leuchars
XW903   XX456   XZ324   XZ341

6 Flight (V)   Gazelle AH.1   RAF Shawbury
XZ304   XZ309   XZ311   XZ335

8 Flight   Gazelle AH.1   Hereford
Also operates the Agusta A.109A, see page 130.
XX379   XZ314

12 Flight   Gazelle AH.1   RAF Brüggen, Germany
XX371   XX386   XZ291   XZ295

16 Flight   Gazelle AH.1   Dhekelia, Cyprus
XZ323   ZB667   ZB679   ZB690

25 Flight   Gazelle AH.1   Belize
This Flight is also due receive Lynx AH.7s from May 1997, see page 139.
ZA734   ZA735

AAC Flight BATU   Gazelle AH.1   Suffield, Canada
British Army Training Unit, field exercise detachment.
XZ340   ZA736   ZB671   ZB677   ZB693

Below: Gazelle AH.1 of 658 Squadron (Volunteers), see page 133.

LYNX AH.7 and AH.9

Specification (AH.7):

Powerplant: Two Rolls-Royce Gem 42-1 turbo-shafts each of 1,135shp (846kW).

Performance: Max speed 161mph (259km/h). Typical combat radius 336 miles (540km).

Weights: Empty 5,683lb (2,578kg). Max take-off 10,750lb (4,876kg).

Dimensions: Rotor diameter 42ft 0in (12.80m). Length 39ft 6¾in (12.06m). Height 11ft 6in (3.50m).

Armament: Eight TOW anti-tank missiles, pintle-mounted machine gun in side door. Up to 12 fully equipped troops, or 2,000lb (907kg) of internal freight or 3,000lb (1,361kg) underslung load.

Manufacturer: Westland Helicopters, Yeovil (with Aérospatiale – now Eurocopter – as sub-contractor). Production complete. Production of the naval Super Lynx for export continuing.

Roles & Variants: General purpose battlefield transport and anti-tank (AH.7) and specialist battlefield transport (AH.9) helicopter. Initial Army version was the AH.1, first flown in 1977, small number upgraded to AH.5 interim standard, but the AH.7 is now the norm. AH.9 fleet includes eight conversions from the AH.7 plus new-build.

First entered service: 1977 (AH.1), 1991 (AH.9).

Colour scheme: Grey/green overall camouflage.

Notes: Because 9 Regiment are currently providing helicopters for the SFOR detachment in Bosnia there is considerable interchange between squadrons (aircrews are currently being provided by 4 Regiment at Wattisham).

See also: Fleet Air Arm and the Royal Marines also operates the Lynx extensively, see page 110. See also 'Test & Trials' (page 143).

Lynx AH.7 of 669 Squadron (see page 139).

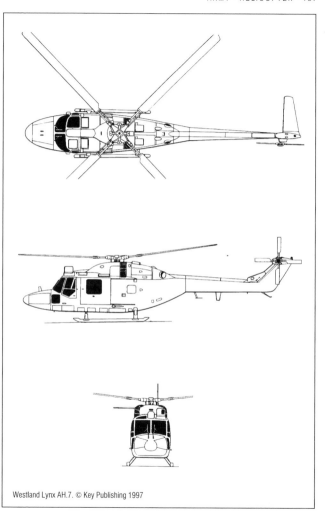

Westland Lynx AH.7. © Key Publishing 1997

651 Squadron   **Lynx AH.7**   **Gütersloh, Germany**
Unit also operates the Gazelle AH.1, see page 133.
XZ219   XZ221   XZ674

652 Squadron   **Lynx AH.7**   **Gütersloh, Germany**
Unit also operates the Gazelle AH.1, see page 133.
XZ196   XZ665   XZ680

653 Squadron   **Lynx AH.9**   **Wattisham**
ZF538   ZG886   ZG887   ZG888   ZG889   ZG914   ZG915
ZG919   ZG920   ZG922   ZG923

654 Squadron   **Lynx AH.7**   **Wattisham**
Unit also operates the Gazelle AH.1, see page 133.
XZ179   XZ194   XZ211   XZ220

655 Squadron   **Lynx AH.7**   **Aldergrove**
One coded aircraft is a 'remnant' from a previous unit.
XZ172   XZ174   XZ198   XZ205   XZ215   XZ218   XZ615
XZ647   XZ649   O:XZ655   XZ662   XZ663   XZ672   XZ673
ZD273   ZE379   ZE381

656 Squadron   **Lynx AH.7**   **Dishforth**
Unit also operates the Gazelle AH.1, see page 133.
XZ171   XZ208   XZ617   XZ646   XZ679   ZD274

657 Squadron   **Lynx AH.1**   **Dishforth**
Unit also operates the Gazelle AH.1, see page 133.
XZ199   XZ214   XZ222   XZ608   XZ616   XZ651

659 Squadron   **Lynx AH.9**   **Wattisham**
Single-digit codes in black on the fuselage.
1:ZE382   2:ZE375   3:ZE380   4:ZE376   5:ZF539   6:ZF540   7:ZG885
8:ZG916   9:ZG917   10:ZG918   11:ZG921

661 Squadron   **Lynx AH.7**   **Gütersloh, Germany**
Unit also operates the Gazelle AH.1, see page 133. Only one Lynx currently confirmed.
XZ666

662 Squadron   **Lynx AH.7**   **Wattisham**
Unit also operates the Gazelle AH.1, see page 133.
XZ188   XZ206   XZ641   XZ669

663 Squadron **Lynx AH.7** **Wattisham**
One coded aircraft is a 'remnant' from a previous unit. Unit also operates the Gazelle AH.1, see page 133.
H:ZD284 XZ185 XZ197

664 Squadron **Lynx AH.7** **Dishforth**
Unit also operates the Gazelle AH.1, see page 133.
XZ212 XZ648 XZ653 XZ664 XZ670 ZD276

667 Squadron **Lynx AH.7** **Middle Wallop**
Unit also operates the Gazelle AH.1, see page 133.
XZ187 XZ606

669 Squadron **Lynx AH.7** **Wattisham**
Unit also operates the Gazelle AH.1, see page 133.
XZ173 XZ176 XZ207 ZD277

671 Squadron **Lynx AH.7** **Middle Wallop**
Unit also due to operate the Gazelle AH.1, see page 133. The unit also is the Army Air Corps display team, the 'Blue Eagles'. Single-letter codes in black on the fuselage.
A:ZD278 C:ZD279 E:XZ675 H:ZD272 I:XZ193 K:ZD281
N:XZ676 P:ZD283 T:XZ652 Z:XZ175

25 Flight **Lynx AH.7** **Belize**
Due to receive Lynx AH.7s from May 1997, in addition to the Gazelles - see page 133.

Below: Lynx AH.9 of 659 Squadron (see page 138).

SQUIRREL HT.1 and HT.2

Specification:
Powerplant: One Turboméca Arriel turboshaft of 616shp (459kW).
Performance: Maximum speed 144mph (232km/h). Range, no reserves 435 miles (700km).
Weights: Empty 2,348lb (1,065kg). Max take-off 4,300lb (1,950kg).
Dimensions: Rotor diameter 35ft 0¾in (10.69m). Length 35ft 9½in (10.91m). Height 10ft 4in (3.15m).

Manufacturer: Eurocopter, Marignane, France. Deliveries to DHFS and 670 Squadron due to be completed 1997, production for other customers continuing.

Role & Variants: Training helicopter. Manufacturer's designation AS.350B and known as the Ecureuil (= Squirrel) in France and the A-Star in the USA. HT.1 for basic training, HT.2 for advanced instrument/night vision goggle and operational training.

First entered service: 1997.

Notes: HT.1s operated within the Defence Helicopter Flying School (run by FBS Ltd, a combined operation by FR Aviation, Bristow Helicopters and SERCO) to train helicopter pilots for all three services. DHFS officially came into operation at Shawbury, Shropshire, on 1st April 1997. HT.2s to be operated by 670 Squadron from Middle Wallop.

Colour scheme: Gloss black fuselage with gloss yellow engine bay.

See also: Respective DHFS entries for the RAF and Fleet Air Arm, pages 58 and 120. The RAF also operates the essentially similar Twin Squirrel, see page 68 for details and the broadly similar three-view.

660 Squadron Squirrel HT.1 RAF Shawbury

'Last two' of serial on nose and fuselage side. No.660 is the 'shadow' squadron for the AAC within the Defence Helicopter Flying School from 1st April 1997 notionally looking after basic training. See 'Notes' above. The first example, civilian registered as G-BXAG, illustrated below, became ZJ255.

ZJ255 ZJ256 ZJ257 ZJ258 ZJ259 ZJ260 ZJ261 ZJ262 ZJ263 ZJ264
ZJ265 ZJ266 ZJ267 ZJ268 ZJ269 ZJ270 ZJ271 ZJ272 ZJ273 ZJ274
ZJ275 ZJ276 ZJ277 ZJ278 ZJ279 ZJ280

670 Squadron Squirrel HT.2 Middle Wallop

Will receive eight HT.2s during 1997, balance will be based at Shawbury with DHFS. Also operates the Gazelle AH.1, see page 132. See 'Notes' above.

ZJ243 ZJ244 ZJ245 ZJ246 ZJ247 ZJ248 ZJ249 ZJ250 ZJ251 ZJ252
ZJ253 ZJ254

ISLANDER AL.1

Specification:

Powerplant: Two Allison 250-B17C turboprops each of 320shp (238.5kW).

Performance: Max speed 196mph (315km/h). Range 838 miles (1,349km).

Weights: Empty 4,220lb (1,914kg). Max take-off 7,000lb (3,175kg).

Dimensions: Span 49ft 0in (14.94m). Length 35ft 7¾in (10.86m). Height 13ft 8¾in (4.18m).

Manufacturer: Airframe manufactured by IAv Bucuresti in Romania under licence to Pilatus Britten-Norman Ltd, Bembridge, Isle of Wight, who complete to customer requirements.

Roles & Variants: Light transport and special duties surveillance aircraft. Has 'plumbing' for two under-wing hard points. (Manufacturer's designation BN-2T Turbine Defender.)

First entered service: 1989.

Colour scheme: Low visibility grey overall.

See also: Islander CC.2 and CC.2A (page 46) and 'Test & Trials' (page 143).

1 Flight		Islander AL.1		Aldergrove	
ZG844	ZG846	ZG847	ZG848	ZG993	ZG994

Advanced Fixed Wing Flight   **Islander AL.1**   **Middle Wallop**
ZG845

HISTORIC

Army Air Corps Historic Aircraft Flight   Middle Wallop

In addition to the aircraft operated by the Flight, the Reserve Collection Trust* has acquired aircraft to back-up and support the activities of the Flight

Alouette AH.2	XR379	
Auster AOP.9	XP242*	(G-BUCI)
	XR244	
Beaver AL.1	XP772*	(G-BUCJ), under restoration
	XP820	
Scout AH.1	Q:XT626	
Sioux AH.1	B:XT131	
Skeeter AOP.12	XL814	illustrated below
Tiger Moth	N6985*	(G-AHMN)
	G-AOHY*	under restoration

TEST & TRIALS

MINISTRY OF DEFENCE TEST FLEETS

Many of the types operated in this sector are current service types and further technical details can be found in the appropriate section of the book with page references given in brackets. For out of service or other types a greater type designation is given.

Defence Evaluation & Research Agency (DERA):

Aircraft Test & Evaluation Sectors (ATES) DTEO Boscombe Down
Divided into the following : Combat Aircraft; Patrol and Support Aircraft; Rotary Wing.

Harrier GR.7, T.10* (p.8)	ZD318, ZD319, ZH653*	
(Hawker) Hunter FGA.9	XE601	
Jaguar GR.1A, T.2* (p.12)	XX979	ZB615*
Tornado GR.1 (p.16)	ZA402	B-53:ZA353
Tornado F.2 (p.24)	ZA267	
Chinook HC.2 (p.54)	BN:ZA718	
Sea King HC.4, HAS.6* (p.114)	ZF115	XZ576*

Empire Test Pilots School (ETPS)		**DTEO Boscombe Down**
(HS) Andover C.1	XS606	illustrated above
(BAC) One-Eleven 479	ZE432	
(Beagle) Basset CC.1	XS743	
Gazelle HT.2 (p.108)	XZ936	XZ939
Hawk T.1 (p.84)	1:XX341	2:XX342
(Hawker) Hunter T.7	4:XL564	2:XL612
Jaguar T.2A (p.12)	XX145	XX830
Lynx Mk.7 (p.136)	ZD560	
Tucano T.1 (p.92)	ZF510	ZF511

School of Aviation Medicine (SAM)   **DTEO Boscombe Down**

Hawk T.1 (p.84)   XX162   XX327

Meteorological Research Flight (MRF)   **DTEO Boscombe Down**

Hercules W.2 (p.44)   XV208

Defence Research Agency (DRA) Experimental Flying Squadron
                                               DTEO Boscombe Down

(BAC) One-Eleven	XX105 (Srs 201), illustrated above
	XX919 (Srs 402)
	ZE433 (Srs 479, operated by Ferranti for Eurofighter radar development)
	ZH763 (Srs 539)
(HS) Andover C.1, C.1PR*, CC.2+	XS596* XS646 XS790+
HS.748 Series 107	XW750
(EE) Canberra B.6	XH567
(EE) Canberra B(I).8	WT327
Harrier T.4 (p.8)	XW175 (VAAC trials aircraft)
(North American) Harvard T.2B	KF183
(Hawker) Hunter T.7	WV383
Jaguar GR.1A (p.12)	06:XX117
Lynx Mk.5X, AH.5* (p.136)	ZD285* ZD559
(Piper) Navajo Chieftain 350	ZF622
Sea King Mk.4X (p.114)	ZB506
Tornado GR.1 (p.16)	ZA326
Tornado F.2 (p.24)	ZD902
Wessex HC.2 (p.70)	XR503

Ministry of Defence (Procurement Executive)

Aircraft are allocated as required during trials.

Air & Sea Capabilities Sectors

(EE) Canberra B.2
Hawk T.1 (p.84)
(Gloster) Meteor D.16
(Piper) Navajo Chieftain 350

Jetstream T.2 (p.124)

Manufacturers Fleets

British Aerospace (BAe)

Harrier GR.7, T.10* (p.8)

Sea Harrier F/A2 (p.102)
BAe (HS).125-600B

British Aerospace (BAe)

Eurofighter 2000
Hawk T.1 (p.84)
Hawk Mk.50, Mk.102D*
Hawk Mk.200RDA
Jaguar GR.1A
(Pilatus) PC-9
Tornado GR.1 (p.16)
Tornado GR.4 (p.23)
Tornado F.2, F.3* (p.24)

DTEO Boscombe Down

DTEO Llanbedr

WH734	WK128	
XX154	XX160	DS:XX170
Z:WK800	L:WH453 (stored)	
ZF521		

DTEO West Freugh
XX475

Dunsfold, Surrey

ZD318	ZD319	ZD321	ZD436
ZH653*			
ZA195			
ZF130			

Warton, Lancs

ZH588	ZH590	
XX177		
ZA101	ZJ100	
ZJ201		
XX719		
ZG969, illustrated above		
ZA327	ZA328	ZA354
XZ631	ZG773	ZD708
ZA283	ZD899	ZE155*

Martin-Baker
(Gloster) Meteor T.7

Pilatus Britten-Norman
(PBN) ASTOR Islander (p.46)

Slingsby Sailplanes
Viking TX.1 (p94)

Westland Helicopters
(Westland/Sikorsky WS-70)
  Black Hawk
EHI EH-101
EHI Merlin HM1
Lynx AH.7, AH.9* (p.136)
Lynx HMA8 (p.110)

Chalgrove, Oxon
WL419, illustrated above

Bembridge, Isle of Wight
ZG989

Kirbymoorside, Yorks
ZE686

Yeovil, Somerset
ZG468

ZF641	ZF649	ZH647	ZJ116
ZH821	ZH822		
XZ170	ZG884*		
XZ236	ZD267		

THE FUTURE

As *Air Forces UK* closed for press, the newly-elected Labour government, via Defence Minister George Robertson, announced a Strategic Defence Review to run from late May until probably November 1997 to examine 'the role, structure and equipment programmes of the [UK's] armed forces'. While programmes already on contract looked not to be at risk, it seems inevitable that there will be a major shake-up.

In June 1997 George Robertson and the Prime Minister, Tony Blair, were seeking assurances by the German government relating to their commitment to the production phase of the Eurofighter 2000 (illustrated page 143, see also page 146). Germany, Italy, Spain and the UK are in collaboration on this prestigious fighter programme. For a detailed examination of the programme, see *Eurofighter 200: Europe's Fighter for the New Millennium* by Hugh Harkins and published by our sister organisation, Aerofax.

Work is currently getting underway at Bournemouth, Dorset and Warton, Lancs, on the Nimrod 2000 (MR.4?) programme, a re-engined, re-equipped and almost rebuilt version of the MR.2 (see page 32). During February 1997 the first MR.2 fuselages were flown, care of an Antonov An-124 to Bournemouth for initial work to be undertaken. At present the plans are that 21 of the fleet will be upgraded with service entry set for 2002.

The RAF also has what is best described a form of commitment to the European Future Large Aircraft (FLA) airlifter, being developed under the aegis of the Airbus consortium (see top, right). Along with the Hercules C.4 and C.5 (see page 45), the FLA would form a mixed transport fleet meeting the RAF's tactical and strategic needs. By mid-1997 the future prospects for FLA were looking a little rosier...

Also from the military wing of Airbus and perhaps likely to fare better is a proposal to replace the VC-10 tanker fleet (page 50) earlier than expected – they were planned to serve on until *circa* 2010 – with Airbus A310 MRTTs (multi-role tanker/transports) perhaps through a radical 'COMO' (see page 4) agreement. Boeing is also courting the RAF with its military 767 version.

Both the RAF and the Fleet Air Arm have ordered the Anglo-Italian EHI (GKN-Westland and Agusta) EH.101 Merlin heavy helicopter (see middle, right). The Navy has ordered 44 HM1s for anti-submarine warfare, replacing ultimately the Westland Sea King (see page 114) in that role. It is possible that transport and other versions will be adopted by the FAA. (HM1s will be ZH821 to ZH864, first deliveries in 1998. See also 'Test & Trials', page 143, for prototypes.) The RAF is to take 22 Merlins (ZJ117 to ZJ138, apparently designated HC.3s) to replace the Puma (page 60) with first deliveries occurring in 1999.

The Army Air Corps has chosen the McDonnell Douglas AH-64D Longbow Apache as its next anti-tank helicopter (see page 136). The first eight will be built in the USA, the remainder under licence by GKN-Westland as the WAH-64D. (Serials ZJ166 to ZJ233. Initial operations will take place in the year 2000.

Further away, the UK is a full partner in the US Joint Strike Fighter (JSF) programme in which a Lockheed Martin led team and another from Boeing are preparing concept demonstration aircraft. The Royal Navy sees the JSF as the replacement for the Sea Harrier FA2 and the RAF is maintaining a 'watching brief' on the programme.

UNITED STATES FORCES IN THE UK

48th Fighter Wing
492nd Fighter Squadron
Blue fin-tip, tail code 'LN'.

RAF Lakenheath
F-15E Eagle

90-0248	90-0251	90-0255	90-0256	90-0257	90-0258	90-0259
90-0260	90-0261	90-0262	91-0300	91-0301	91-0302	91-0303
91-0304	91-0305	91-0307	91-0308	91-0309	91-0310	91-0311
91-0312	91-0325	91-0326	91-0329	91-0332		

493rd Fighter Squadron
Yellow fin-tip, tail code 'LN'.

F-15C and 'D* Eagle

86-0147	86-0154	86-0156	86-0159	86-0160	86-0163	86-0164
86-0165	86-0166	86-0167	86-0169	86-0171	86-0172	86-0173
86-0174	86-0175	86-0176	86-0178	86-0180	86-0182*	

494th Fighter Squadron
Red fin-tip, tail code 'LN'.

F-15E Eagle

91-0306	91-0313	91-0314	91-0315	91-0316	91-0317	91-0318
91-0319	91-0320	91-0321	91-0322	91-0323	91-0324	91-0327
91-0328	91-0330	91-0331	91-0333	91-0334	91-0335	91-0601
91-0602	91-0603	91-0604	91-0605	92-0364		

Below, F-15C Eagle of the 493rd Fighter Squadron, 48th Fighter Wing.

100th Air Refueling Wing   **RAF Mildenhall**
351st Air Refueling Squadron   **KC-135R Stratotanker**
White 'D' in black square on the fin (a throwback to the unit's days as the 100th Bombardment
Group flying B-17 Flying Fortresses).

57-1439	57-1456	57-1474	57-1499	57-1506	59-1482	61-0312
62-3517	62-3538					

352nd Special Operations Group   **RAF Mildenhall**
7th Special Operations Squadron   **MC-130H Hercules**

84-0476	86-1699	87-0023	88-0193	88-0194

21st Special Operations Squadron **MH-53J**
'Pave Low III' enhanced variant.
67-14993   68-10924   69-5790   70-1625   70-1626   73-1648

67th Special Operations Squadrons **C-130E*, MC-130P**
63-7814*   69-5819   69-5820   69-5823   69-5826   69-5831

Naval Air Facility Mildenhall **UC-12J** **RAF Mildenhall**
Tail code '8G'.
163837   163840   163843

MILITARY AIRFIELDS

There follows a listing of current UK mainland and overseas airfields holding units mentioned within the text. This is not designed as a precise locator for the airfields, but to help the reader see what units are to be found by location. Column two gives the 'ownership' details of the airfield (Pte = private); column three gives general location and column four lists units in the order the book is presented (ie RAF, FAA, AAC, 'Test & Trials', US).

Aberporth	DTEO	near Cardigan, Dyfed	RAF: 636 VGS, MoD: A&SCS
Abingdon	Army	near Abingdon, Oxon	612 VGS
Akrotiri	RAF	Cyprus	84
Aldergrove	RAF	Belfast Int Airport, NI	RAF: 72, 230, AAC: 655, 665, 1 Flt
Arbroath	RM	near the town, Tayside	662 VGS
Barkston Heath	RAF	near Grantham, Lincs	JEFTS
Belfast City	Pte	Belfast City Airport, NI	664 VGS
Belize City	Pte	Belize	25 Flt
Bembridge	PBN	Isle of Wight	Pilatus Britten-Norman test
Benson	RAF	near Wallingford, Oxon	33, London UAS, Oxford UAS
Boscombe Down	DTEO	near Salisbury, Wilts	RAF: S'ton UAS, SAOEU, MoD: ATES, ETPS, SAM, MRF, DRA-EFS, MoD(PE)
Boulmer	RAF	near Alnwick, Northumberland	202
Bournemouth	Pte	Bournemouth Airport, Dorset	FR Aviation
Brize Norton	RAF	near Witney, Oxon	10, 101, 216
Brüggen	RAF	Germany	RAF: 9, 14, 17, 31, AAC: 12 Flt
Brunei	AAC	Brunei	7 Flt
Cambridge	Pte	Cambridge Airport, Cambs	Cambridge UAS
Catterick	Army	near Richmond, Yorks	645 VGS
Chivenor	RM	near Barnstaple, Devon	22, 624 VGS
Church Fenton	RAF	near Selby, Yorks	Yorkshire UAS
Chalgrove	M-B	near Wallingford, Oxon	Martin-Baker test
Colerne	RAF	near Bath, Glos	Bristol UAS
Coltishall	RAF	near Norwich, Norfolk	6, 41, 54
Coningsby	RAF	near Woodhall Spa, Lincs	5, 29, 56, F3 OEU, BBMF
Cosford	RAF	near Albrighton, Shropshire	Birm' UAS, 633 VGS
Cottesmore	RAF	near Oakham, Leics	TTTE
Cranwell	RAF	near Sleaford, Lincs	45, 55, 3 FTS, CFS, Red Arrows
Culdrose	FAA	near Helston, Cornwall	706, 750, 771, 810, 814, 820, 849, FRADU
Dhekelia	AAC	Cyprus	16 Flt
Dishforth	AAC	near Ripon, Yorks	656, 657, 664
Dunsfold	BAe	near Cranleigh, Surrey	BAe test
Fleetlands	FAA	near Gosport, Hants	NARO Flt
Glasgow	Pte	Glasgow Airport, Strathclyde	Glasgow UAS
Gütersloh	Army	Germany	651, 652, 661
Halton	RAF	near Aylesbury, Bucks	613 VGS
Henlow	RAF	near Stotfold, Beds	616 VGS
Hereford	Army	south west of city, Herefordshire	8 Flt
Hullavington	Army	near Malmesbury, Wilts	621 VGS, 625 VGS
Kenley	RAF	near Caterham, London	615 VGS
Kinloss	RAF	near Forres, Grampian	42, 120, 201, 206, 663 VGS

Kirbymoorside	Pte	near Pickering, Yorks	Slingsby test
Kirknewton	Army	near Currie, Lothian	661 VGS
Laarbruch	RAF	Germany	3, 4
Lakenheath	USAF	near Brandon, Suffolk	48th FW
Leconfield	Army	near Beverley, Yorks	202
Leeming	RAF	near Bedale, Yorks	11, 25, 100, JFACS&TU, Northum' UAS
Leuchars	RAF	near St Andrews, Fife	RAF: 43, 111, Aberdeen UAS, E Lowlands UAS, AAC: 3 Flt
Linton-on-Ouse	RAF	near Haxby, Yorks	1 FTS, 642 VGS
Little Rissington	Army	near Bourton-on-the-Water, Glos	637 VGS
Llanbedr	DTEO	near Harlech, Gwynedd	A&SCS
Lossiemouth	RAF	near Elgin, Grampian	12, 15, 16, 202, 617
Lyneham	RAF	near Wootton Bassett, Wilts	24, 30, 4757, 70
Manston	RAF	near Ramsgate, Kent	617 VGS
Marham	RAF	near Swaffam, Norfolk	2, 13, 39
Middle Wallop	AAC	near Stockbridge, Hants	667, 670, 671, AFWF, AACHAF
Mildenhall	USAF	north of Newmarket, Suffolk	100th ARW, 352nd SOG, NAF
Mount Pleasant	RAF	Falklands Islands	78, 1312 Flt, 1435 Flt
Netheravon	AAC	north of Amesbury, Wilts	658, 666
Newton	RAF	near Nottingham, Notts	RAF: E Midlands UAS, Tri-service: JEFTS
Northolt	RAF	near Ruislip, London	32, Northolt Stn Flt
Odiham	RAF	near Alton, Hants	7, 18, 27
Portland	FAA	near Weymouth, Dorset	702, 815
Predannack	FAA	near Mullion, Cornwall	626 VGS
Prestwick	FAA	Prestwick Airport, Strathclyde	819
Roborough	Pte	Plymouth Airport, Devon	NFGF, Bond Helicopters/FOT
St Athan	RAF	near Barry, Glamorgan	Wales UAS, St Athan Stn Flt, 634 VGS
St Mawgan	RAF	near Newquay, Cornwall	22, 203
Samlesbury	BAe	near Preston, Lancs	635 VGS
Sealand	RAF	near Queensferry, Clwyd	631 VGS
Shawbury	RAF	near Shrewsbury, Shrop	RAF: 60, FAA: 705, AAC: 660, 6 Flt, Tri-service: DHFS
Suffield	Army	Canada	BATU
Syerston	RAF	near Newark-on-Trent, Notts	CGS, 643 VGS, 644 VGS
Tees-side	Pte	Tees-side Airport, Durham	FR Aviation
Ternhill	Army	near Market Drayton, Shrop	632 VGS
Topcliffe	Army	near Thirsk, Yorks	CFS
Upavon	Army	north of Amesbury, Wilts	622 VGS
Valley	RAF	near Holyhead, Anglesey	19, 22, 74, 208, 4 FTS
Waddington	RAF	near Lincoln, Lincs	8, 23, 51
Warton	BAe	near Lytham St Anne's, Lancs	BAe test
Wattisham	AAC	near Stowmarket, Suffolk	RAF: 22, AAC: 653, 654, 659, 662, 663, 669
Watton	Army	east of the town, Norfolk	611 VGS
West Freugh	DTEO	near Stranraer, Dumfries	A&SCS
Wethersfield	MoD Police	near Braintree, Essex	614 VGS
Wittering	RAF	near Stamford, Lincs	1, 20
Woodvale	RAF	near Southport, Merseyside	Liverpool UAS, Manchester UAS
Yeovil	WHL	west of the town, Somerset	GKN-Westland test
Yeovilton	FAA	near Ilchester, Somerset	800, 801, 845, 846, 847, 848, 899, FONA, Heron Stn Flt, RNHF

We hope that you have enjoyed this Midland Publishing book.
Our titles are carefully edited and designed for you by a knowledgeable and enthusiastic team of specialists, with over 20 years of experience. Further titles are in the course of preparation but we would welcome ideas on what you would like to see. If you have a manuscript or project that requires publishing, we should be happy to consider it; brief details initially, please.

In addition, our associate company, Midland Counties Publications, offer an exceptionally wide range of aviation and railway books/videos for sale by mail-order around the world. For a copy of the appropriate catalogue, please write, telephone or fax to:
**Midland Counties Publications, Unit 3 Maizefield, Hinckley Fields, Hinckley, Leics, LE10 1YF.
Tel: 01455 233747; Fax: 01455 233737.
E-mail: midlandbooks@compuserve.com**

BRITISH AIRFIELD BUILDINGS OF WWII
Aviation Pocket Guide 1

Graham Buchan Innes

The world of airfield buildings is one of constant fascination to enthusiasts. Until now, references on this subject have been the domain of very specialist works, or to be partially found within high price books. All of this has conspired to put off a whole army of people who have a thirst for such knowledge.

British Airfield Buildings is the answer to this need and in a genuinely pocket-size form. From control towers, to hangars, to defensive strongpoints,

barrack blocks, maintenance buildings to the humble latrine, it provides an illustration of a *surviving* example, highlighting details and other styles of similar building.

Over 200 illustrations with brief but informative captions take the reader for an excursion through a typical wartime station.

British Airfield Buildings provides an ideal primer to a subject close to the heart of all enthusiasts.

Softback
148 x 105 mm, 128 pages
230 b/w photographs
1 85780 026 5
£5.95

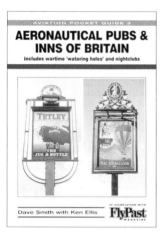

AERONAUTICAL PUBS & INNS OF BRITAIN
Aviation Pocket Guide 3

Dave Smith with Ken Ellis

There can be few more perfect combinations than aircraft and pubs. Aviation enthusiasts all over the UK have a passion for both. An amazing number of public houses and inns have strong aeronautical connections.

The *Air Balloon* at Birdlip was a venue for Edwardian ballooning adventures; the *Sir Frank Whittle* in Lutterworth is close to where the first British jet engine ran; the *Bader Arms* was opened by the famous Battle of Britain fighter pilot; and the *Double O Two* near Bristol celebrates the first British-built Concorde.

There is a great fascination in these inns, their signs and their significance, but this book also takes the interest to a much overlooked area – watering holes. All major bomber and fighter stations had favourite places for their airmen to go and unwind.

Topping off a fascinating study is a look at the growing number of aircraft to be found adorning night clubs! A gazetteer of existing aeronautical pubs and inns completes this absorbing guide.

Softback
148 x 105 mm, 96 pages
92 b/w, 3 colour photos, 5 cartoons
1 85780 048 6
£5.95

DISCOVER
AVIATION TRAILS
Aviation Pocket Guide 4

Paul Shaw

Interest in aviation museums, airfields used and disused, memorials and other aeronautical venues has never been higher. Enthusiasts are keen to know what to look for and how. Until now, their plans to tour the country relied very much on their own researches – with the risk of missing many 'gems'.

Now an answer is to hand in the popular Aviation Pocket Guide format, a pocket sized collection of twelve regional tours that can be undertaken by car in a day, or over a weekend with 'add ons'. The suggested tours span the country, offering enthusiasts a 'local' to investigate and a many possibilities to be taken up on holiday: Cornwall; Derbyshire/Leicestershire/ Notts; Essex; Lincoln; Lincolnshire; London; Manchester and Cheshire; Norfolk; Northamptonshire; Southern Scotland; South Wales; Yorkshire.

With each tour come plenty of suggestions, each carefully put together to allow for a 'gentle' pace. An ideal travelling companion for enthusiasts of all ages.

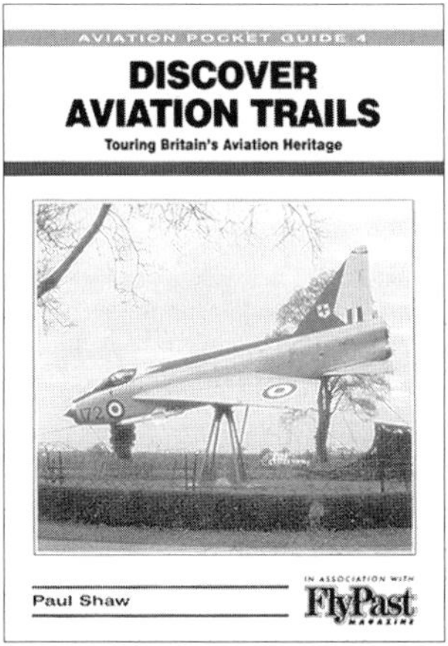

AVIATION POCKET GUIDE 4

DISCOVER
AVIATION TRAILS
Touring Britain's Aviation Heritage

Paul Shaw

IN ASSOCIATION WITH
FlyPast
MAGAZINE

Softback
148 x 105 mm, 128 pages
97 b/w, 3 colour photos, 12 maps
1 85780 049 4
£5.95

HIGH GROUND
WRECKS & RELICS
Aviation Pocket Guide 5

David J Smith

David J Smith

Interest in the aviation heritage of Britain
and Ireland has never been higher and
enthusiasts always strive for 'new'
territory. *High Ground Wrecks & Relics*
fosters an extension of the already well-
established 'wreck-hunting' hobby, by
taking readers up into the hills and
mountains.

An astonishing number of aircraft that
have crashed into high ground remain as
stark monuments to wartime and
peacetime errors and misfortunes.

The book carefully charts the major
mountain sites and describes the aircraft
remains to be found, plus fascinating
insights into their history. Map
references and suggestions about fell
and mountain walking add to the
potential.

For those that do not wish to combine
aviation history with exercise, *High
Ground Wrecks & Relics* is a superb
reference source of the fates of a wide
variety of aircraft. In either case, its
pocket size, handy tables and
explanatory narrative will be a boon to
enthusiasts. A new and completely
revised edition of a popular 'standard'

Softback
148 x 105 mm, 96 pages
52 black and white photos
1 85780 070 2
£6.95

Military Aviation Review

To help readers to keep up to date with the latest changes in *Air Forces UK*, a subscription to the journal *Military Aviation Review* is essential. At least 40 pages, A5-sized with illustrations, monthly provides coverage of the latest news, visitors, airshow reports and advanced information on exercises and deployments. Contact MAP at the address below for a sample copy.

The majority of the photographs in *Air Forces UK* were supplied by Military Aircraft Photographs – MAP. Every month, MAP produces a listing with over 2,000 different photographs in colour and black and White, military and civil, contemporary and archive. MAP provides coverage of all major military airshows in both the UK and abroad and the permanent catalogue lists over 250,000 photos and available on computer disc. Contact the address below for the current monthly list and free sample photos.

Military Aircraft Photographs, Aslackby, Sleaford, Lincolnshire, NG34 0HG. Tel: 01778 440760. Fax: 01778 440060. E-mail brianmap@btinternet.com